Lent with St Benedict

Lent with St Benedict

Bede Frost

Kevin
Mayhew

This edition first published in 1997 by
KEVIN MAYHEW LTD
Rattlesden
Bury St Edmunds
Suffolk IP30 0SZ

0 1 2 3 4 5 6 7 8 9

ISBN 1 84003 104 2
Catalogue No 1500155

Front cover: *St Benedict* by Andrea di Bartolo (1189-1428).
Reproduced by kind permission of Christie's,
London/Bridgeman Art library, London
Cover design by Graham Johnstone
Edited by Mark Jabalé and Michael Forster
Typesetting by Louise Hill
Printed and bound in Great Britain

CONTENTS

FOREWORD 9

ASH WEDNESDAY
The observance of Lent 11

FIRST THURSDAY IN LENT
The task of Lent 15

FIRST FRIDAY IN LENT
The purpose of Lent 18

FIRST SATURDAY IN LENT
The offering of Lent 20

FIRST SUNDAY IN LENT
The practices of Lent 23

MONDAY OF THE FIRST WEEK IN LENT
The nature and character of the Holy Rule 27

TUESDAY OF THE FIRST WEEK IN LENT
The school of Jesus Christ 30

WEDNESDAY OF THE FIRST WEEK IN LENT
The sloth of disobedience 33

THURSDAY OF THE FIRST WEEK IN LENT
The fact of God 36

FRIDAY OF THE FIRST WEEK IN LENT
The fact a fact to us 39

SATURDAY OF THE FIRST WEEK IN LENT
The presence of God 42

SECOND SUNDAY IN LENT
The urgency of the call of God 46

MONDAY OF THE SECOND WEEK IN LENT
The fear of God 49

TUESDAY OF THE SECOND WEEK IN LENT
The end for which we are created 52

WEDNESDAY OF THE SECOND WEEK IN LENT
The vision of God 55

THURSDAY OF THE SECOND WEEK IN LENT
Renouncing our own will 58

FRIDAY OF THE SECOND WEEK IN LENT
The strong weapons of obedience 62

SATURDAY OF THE SECOND WEEK IN LENT
There is a war on 66

THIRD SUNDAY IN LENT
Christ, our true King 70

MONDAY OF THE THIRD WEEK IN LENT
Our enemies, and how to meet them 74

TUESDAY OF THE THIRD WEEK IN LENT
Who shall rest upon his holy hill? 77

WEDNESDAY OF THE THIRD WEEK IN LENT
Girded with faith 80

THURSDAY OF THE THIRD WEEK IN LENT
The performance of good works 83

FRIDAY OF THE THIRD WEEK IN LENT
The instruments of good works 86

SATURDAY OF THE THIRD WEEK IN LENT
The love of our neighbour 90

FOURTH SUNDAY IN LENT
What things we must avoid 93

MONDAY OF THE FOURTH WEEK IN LENT
What to fear, and what to hope for 96

TUESDAY OF THE FOURTH WEEK IN LENT
With what are we to serve God – I 99

WEDNESDAY OF THE FOURTH WEEK IN LENT
With what are we to serve God – II 102

THURSDAY OF THE FOURTH WEEK IN LENT
The guidance of the Gospel 105

FRIDAY OF THE FOURTH WEEK IN LENT
Stability and perseverance 108

SATURDAY OF THE FOURTH WEEK IN LENT
Worship 111

PASSION SUNDAY
Prayer 115

MONDAY IN PASSIONTIDE
Study 119

TUESDAY IN PASSIONTIDE
Work 122

WEDNESDAY IN PASSIONTIDE
Zeal, good and bad 126

THURSDAY IN PASSIONTIDE
Humility – I 130

FRIDAY IN PASSIONTIDE
Humility – II 134

SATURDAY IN PASSIONTIDE
Humility – III 138

PALM SUNDAY
Humility – IV 142

Monday in Holy Week
Humility – V 146

Tuesday in Holy Week
Humility – VI 150

Wednesday in Holy Week
Patience – I 153

Maundy Thursday
Patience – II 156

Good Friday
Silence 159

Holy Saturday
Peace 163

References 167

Foreword

When Bede Frost first published his book in 1942 he wrote in his foreword:

> The following pages do not contain a commentary on the Holy Rule of St Benedict, nor do they treat of it from the point of view of a monk. They are readings in those parts of it which concern the Christian living in the world as much as they do the monk in the cloister. To such are they addressed with the hope that a Lent spent under so wise and holy a master may be profitable in causing many to love what he loved and to practise what he taught.

Bede Frost was a Benedictine oblate whose son Edmund, Dom Raymund Frost, joined the community of Nashdom, and then joined Belmont Abbey, where he eventually became Prior. During Edmund's youth, father and son travelled the world over. Bede was an oblate of the community of Nashdom, and had quite a following of young students and artists who used to come to him for spiritual advice. As the following pages will show he was eminently practical and down to earth and, although his writings may sound a little archaic nowadays, the issues that he discusses are just as valid. The style for this publication could have been modernised, but it would not have carried the same conviction; and a great deal of the charm in the way Bede Frost comes across to us would have been lost. However, in the normal course of editing some revisions have been felt necessary to reflect changes in the use of language or in the way we understand the human personality; once or twice, also, Frost referred to contemporary events and circumstances which would not resonate with people today, and here too changes have been made. Great care has been taken, though, in doing this, to remain faithful to the Rule of St Benedict and to the spirit of what Frost wrote.

Monks are human beings; they are subject to the same temptations and weaknesses as people in the world. This book talks as eloquently to both; it is a treasury of solid, helpful advice on how to lead a good Christian life.

MARK JABALÉ O. S. B, ABBOT OF BELMONT.
MICHAEL FORSTER

Ash Wednesday

The observance of Lent

As this book is intended primarily for use during Lent and Passiontide, it may fittingly begin with the consideration of what St Benedict has to say about the observance of this holy season in the forty-ninth chapter of the Rule.

> Although the life of a monk ought at all times to have about it a Lenten observance, yet, since few have strength enough for this, we exhort all, at least during the days of Lent, to keep themselves in all purity of life and to wash away during that holy season the negligences of other times. This we shall worthily accomplish if we refrain from all sin and give ourselves to prayer with tears, to holy reading, compunction of heart, and abstinence. In these days, therefore, let us add something to our usual meed of service, such as private prayer and abstinence from food and drink, so that every one may freely offer to God, with the joy of the Holy Spirit, something above the allotted measure, denying the body somewhat of food, drink, and sleep, talking and laughter, and thus with spiritual joy await the holy feast of Easter.

To this the saint adds the condition that such extra exercises must be undertaken only with the approval of the abbot, since 'what is done without leave of the spiritual father shall be imputed presumption and vainglory, and merit no reward'.

Let us note, first of all, that in this chapter St Benedict is more concerned with the reason for which, and the spirit in which, Lent is to be observed than in the details of that observance, a fact to be kept in mind as we make our Lenten rule. For the most important question concerning any practice of the Christian life is not, 'How shall I do this?' but 'Why am I going to do it?' In other words, it is the end and motive moving and underlying any act which gives to that act its specific worth, making it good, bad, or indifferent. Thus each practice and every activity of the Christian life should bear the relation of a means to an end, must be prompted by something beyond itself, must contribute to that one end which St Benedict defines as 'truly seeking after God', the end not of the monk only but of every Christian. It is true that the immediate end of the Lenten observance is in the words of St Leo the Great (in a sermon on Lent from which St Benedict seems to have drawn the chapter we are considering), that we may celebrate with purified minds and bodies the most excellent passion of the Lord under which term he includes the 'Paschal Feast'. But what is each Easter of this life but a step towards, as it is the foretaste and promise of, that eternal Eastertide in which the faithful soul enters into the joy of the Lord?

We may often wonder why our past Lents, so full of good resolutions and pious practices, seem to have borne so little fruit. May not one reason be that we have not realised and used them as means related to the supreme end and purpose of our lives? That we have expended and exhausted ourselves on practices, seeking satisfaction in them, and so becoming as one who, having plucked the blossom of a fruit tree, foolishly laments that it bears no fruit? Or we have been like a tree which at times so exhausts itself in producing wood and leaves that neither blossom nor fruit appears. Is not this the meaning of the barren fig tree in the Gospel, a figure of a Christian life so dissipated in practices that it bears no fruit to perfection? It was not the curse which our Lord pronounced which prevented its bearing fruit; that was but the recognition of the fact that it had already become incapable of so doing, since all its strength had been spent on producing leaves. Thus covered in leaves it may have presented a more beautiful sight than its neighbours, but it was useless so far as its true purpose was concerned. St Benedict thinks of Lent not so much as a time for adding to our religious exercises as of deepening those which, although necessary at all times, do not embrace or express the whole of life, nor are, for more than one reason, always capable of receiving the same degree of emphasis. 'The life of a monk', and indeed of each Christian, 'ought always to have about it a Lenten observance', say, a Lenten 'character'; but this does not mean that life ought to be a perpetual Lent. 'To everything there is a season, and a time to every purpose . . . a time to weep, and a time to laugh; a time to mourn, and a time to dance; . . . a time to seek, and a time to lose; a time to keep, and a time to cast away; a time to rend, and a time to sew; a time to keep silence, and a time to speak; a time to love, and a time to hate; a time of war, and a time of peace.' Order, proportion, balance are necessary to life: variety must save uniformity from dullness and weariness; uniformity prevents variety from becoming changeableness and inconstancy. The elements of the Christian life are so many and diverse that they cannot all be emphasised at one time, although all exist at once. Just as each season of the liturgical year brings to mind some particular dogma of the faith which, though held as a whole, cannot be seen as a whole, but only in its various parts as they are presented to us, so does each season lay stress upon certain practices, thus enabling us both to keep the proportion of the faith and the due balance of Christian practice.

But St Benedict, being the realist he is, recognises not merely what ought to be but what actually is.

If someone had accused him of not always living up to his profession, I think he would have replied, 'No, nor do I expect to, do you?' 'The life of a monk ought . . .' Yes, but how few have strength enough for this! For Lent involves, as did the forty days of the first Lent in the wilderness, effort, tension, conflict which the frailty of human nature renders, if not impossible, yet dangerous if persisted in beyond our strength. St John would remind us that the bow cannot always be kept taut, and St Teresa, that too much is as bad as too little, no less in religion than in secular affairs. The example of our Lord is sufficient. If he prayed, fasted, taught, and laboured, he also went to wedding feasts and dinner parties, walked with his disciples through the countryside, and loved to visit his friends in the peaceful home at Bethany. It is precisely because the Christian life cannot be lived on a consistently high level, but is a thing of ups and downs, in which the *tempo* varies, that Lent is given to us, not as a disagreeable medicine, though we may need that, but rather as a reviving and strengthening tonic or, to change the metaphor, a course of training by which our whole nature may become more ordered and better fitted to walk worthy of the vocation to which the divine mercy has called us.

First Thursday in Lent

The task of Lent

The specific task of Lent, according to St Benedict, is twofold: to keep oneself in all purity of life, and to wash away the negligences of other times. It is the task of repairing the damage caused by our past inattention and carelessness, and of guarding the interior castle of the soul that it may be kept an inviolate temple of the living God. This combination of repairing and conserving occurs in several of the prayers of Mass, as, for example, in the Post-Communion for the Thursday in the second week of Lent, in which we ask 'that thou mayest restore what thou hast gathered, and preserve what thou hast restored', and again, in the prayer after the sixth Prophecy on the Eve of Pentecost, 'O Lord God of Hosts who repairest what was fallen, and preservest what thou hast repaired'.

But that God will do this depends upon our seeing what needs to be repaired and doing our part in the work required. For God is not a benevolent *genie* who can be invoked to do something for us whilst we sit idly by. We cannot do the work by ourselves, nor, on the other hand, can it be done without ourselves. The fact that 'it is God who worketh in us' does not absolve us from working out 'our own salvation with fear and trembling'; it only assures us that the task is possible in the power of the grace which is given to all who seek it with the intention of using it.

The negligences of the past are washed away by a good confession, which implies that we know what they are and are determined to amend them. But absolution does not remove the effects which our negligences have caused in us. This can be done only by an effort on our part to persist in doing what has been left undone. 'What has fallen' has to be put back, brick by brick as it were, until the tottering wall stands secure again.

Thus the first task of Lent (which, indeed, ought to be done before Lent begins) is to discover what negligences we have been guilty of, and what must be done to repair them. We must try and see, also, what is that 'purity of life' which is to be guarded and preserved; for the aim of the Christian life is not merely negative, to get rid of sin, but positive: the regaining of that integrity, the ordered, balanced, and rightly directed wholeness of our nature which has been injured by sin. Our Lord has told us that merely to 'sweep and garnish' the house of our soul is little worth by itself. It is meant to be occupied, and unless so occupied by its maker and owner, its last state will be worse than the first.

St Benedict frequently uses the words 'purity' and 'pure', not in the restricted sense of physical purity, but in that of the beatitude, 'Blessed are the pure in heart, for they shall see God'. For 'purity of life' is not of the body but of the soul; it is, to quote a modern writer, 'a state of mind, a completeness, an entirety, a possessing of one's own soul'. It is not mere innocence, much less ignorance, or passionlessness, but a condition of being in which the whole of our complex nature is governed and ordered by the dictates of reason and faith. It is essentially of the mind, not of the passions, for as another modern writer makes one of his characters reply to the question, 'Haven't you got any normal appetites?' 'Your appetites depend a great deal upon what you spend your time thinking about'. There can be no purity of life save as founded in, and proceeding from, purity of mind and heart. The citadel of the soul never falls merely from attacks from without, but usually also requires treachery or weakness within opening the gate to the enemy.

Thus our primary effort must be the guard of the mind, that so nothing gains ground there which is contrary to God and the operation of his grace. 'Guard well thy thoughts,' not alone because they are heard in heaven, but because what you habitually think of you will become. Well does the church teach us to pray that we may be given 'the spirit to think and do always such things as be rightful', and 'that by continually thinking upon what is rational, we may accomplish both in word and deed what is pleasing unto thee'.

This does not mean that we must confine our thinking to specifically 'religious' subjects – even if this were possible, which is not the case. So to narrow our thinking would be almost as injurious as to limit it to any other subject. God has created the world for our use, and to use the things of this life well we must think about them rightly. There is nothing puritanical about the saints, however much some of them may have denied themselves the consideration of many things, the essential goodness of which they would never have questioned. And if the Apostle bids us, 'Set your minds on things above', he no less exhorts us to think on 'whatsoever things are true, whatsoever things are honourable, whatsoever things are pure, whatsoever things are lovely, whatsoever things are of good report'.

Thus with our minds full of true and good and lovely thoughts, there will be no room for evil to find a lodging, and we shall keep ourselves 'in all purity of life'. For evil can be overcome only by good, not by a vacuum.

First Friday in Lent

The purpose of Lent

The additions which St Benedict proposes to our normal Christian practice as aids to the worthy accomplishment of our Lenten task may, at first sight, disappoint us. Not only is there no mention of such things as more frequent attendance at Mass (since the Rule does not envisage a daily Mass), nor more frequent reception of Holy Communion, but also nothing is said about sermons or of those various devotions which occupy so large a place in the Lenten exercises of today but which were unknown in the sixth century. Apart from this fact (which is no argument against their existence and use in modern times) it is plain that the saint is thinking of that which lies beneath every practice, the value of which consists in its aiding, conserving and increasing that interior purity of life of which he has spoken. His additions do not consist of new or unwonted practices, but rather are an intensification of normal, common ones. For Lent is no time to decorate ourselves with pious exercises, but one for securing and strengthening the foundations of the spiritual life. Sprinkling holy water about the house will not remedy defective drains, nor painting the exterior do much for one built on the sand.

The apparent simplicity and almost commonplace character of the saint's rules for Lent must not deceive us; they are, in fact, startling and demanding. 'To refrain from all sin.' But is this possible, you ask, when not one of the saints would have claimed to have accomplished it, and the church knows of but one human creature to whom the name 'immaculate' may be applied? Perhaps not; yet, as we sometimes say, there can be no harm in trying; indeed, we are committed to such endeavour already by our baptismal vows. The question is not so much as to its possibility (you never know what you can do until you try) as to its desirability. The fact that it may be extremely doubtful whether we can succeed or not, ought not to, must not, deter us from the attempt. For it is not so much our success which matters as our desire and endeavour.

And whilst no one would be so foolish as to imagine that such an endeavour can be confined to Lent, there is an obvious advantage to be gained in making an unrelenting effort to refrain from all sin during these forty days. For not only does any and every successful effort bring an accession of confidence and strength, but also an effort is more likely to be made, and made better, when a certain time limit is assigned to it. For example, one can envisage the possibility of refraining from all sin for a single day, when to try and imagine it for a week, or longer, would raise doubts which in themselves are likely to contribute to failure. Why not, then, be content humbly to promise, each day of Lent as it comes, to refrain from all sin 'just for today' for after all what more of time is ours than this present day? So, with never any discouragement when we fail, but only penitence, and renewed high resolve, we may, at least, hope for fewer failures than in the past. And who of us, who for these Forty Days had made such a fight, and, without doubt, had had more successes than could have been dreamed of, would not want to go on in humble gratitude and growing, confident courage, throughout the days to come? Those days of Eastertide and beyond, in which the risen Lord becomes more than he had ever been before to us, as, walking by our side in days of reaction and doubt, as once he walked with the two disciples on the way to Emmaus, he whispers to us, 'Peace be unto you. In the world ye shall have tribulations but be of good cheer; I have overcome the world,' and 'My grace is sufficient for thee.'

For Eastertide must not be a going back upon Lent, but the time for gathering and conserving the fruit of Lent.

First Saturday in Lent

The offering of Lent

The Lenten task is to be worthily accomplished, says St Benedict, by giving ourselves to prayer, holy reading, compunction of heart, abstinence, and bodily mortification in the matter of food, drink, sleep, talking and laughter, all of which is to be a personal offering to God, made in the joy of the Holy Spirit. They are to be additions to our normal practice in the sense that, so far as is possible, more time, attention, and care are to be given to them, and this with the special intention of reparation for past negligences and the establishing of ourselves in purity of life. They are additions, also, to what the church orders for all her children and to what an abbot may order in his monastery, and so may and will vary both in quantity and manner with each individual who, whether a religious or layperson, must be guided by the conditions, needs, and possibilities of their particular vocation and occupation.

We may well note here that St Benedict's teaching about asceticism is much more moderate than that of earlier monastic practice, and this because he has a wider and saner view of the purpose it is intended to serve. Body and soul, to him, are not irreconcilable enemies, the former to be crushed to ensure the freedom of the latter, but rather integral parts of one nature, friends which having fallen out with each other need to be reconciled, that each may support and aid the other. If there is need to chastise the body and bring it into subjection, as St Paul says, this is only because it so easily forgets its place and in doing so injures both itself and the soul. But neither can be pampered at the expense of the other, and the aim of Christian asceticism is to heal and strengthen the whole nature, that in a restored integrity of our being we may render our whole self 'a living sacrifice, holy, acceptable unto God'.

Thus, whatever is done in Lent should contribute to this end. So nothing is gained by an excess, whether in prayer or mortification, which leaves us exhausted and fatigued in soul or body, or both, and provokes a reaction when Lent is over which will undo all the good we may have gained. True, the temptation to do too little is stronger than that to exceed our strength and grace; but even a little, done well and persevered in, is preferable to laying a burden upon ourselves which we shall be only too glad to throw off when Lent is over.

We are to see Lent not as a necessary but forbidding thing, like a visit to the dentist, nor as an opportunity for indulging an inordinate love for extra services and a round of sermon tasting. The person who recently said to the writer, 'I am going to four courses this Lent; one here, one at – and two in town,' did not receive, as she did not deserve, the commendation she obviously expected. There are too many people to whom listening to sermons is but a good excuse for not exercising their own minds upon the things of religion, and really putting them into practice. But only what we do think about, not merely hear, has any real influence on our lives.

To those who regard the approach, and demands, of Lent with some dismay, St Benedict would say: You must see it as a joyful offering which of your own will you make to God, an act of generous giving by which, indeed, you become capable of receiving what God would give you. It is our Lord's word, 'Give, and it shall be given you,' 'It is more blessed to give than to receive,' since he 'filleth the hungry with good things'.

Any task which we approach with dislike and annoyance, and perform merely from necessity, will prove to be even more distasteful and difficult than we pictured it. But let the same task be not only calmly but joyfully accepted and offered to God, and its whole character is changed. Is it not true that more joy is gained in doing things for others than in doing them for ourselves, in giving rather than in receiving?

If we come to Lent with our mind centred on the good we expect to receive as a sort of reward for our not very willing compliance with its demands, we shall probably be disappointed. But if we come, beggars as we are, yet with the desire to give generously what lies within our power, assuredly we shall not go empty away. There can be no impoverishment in such giving, for it adds not to God, whose fullness knows no need, but to ourselves who are all need.

'Joy of the Holy Spirit,' 'spiritual joy'. We must understand that this fruit of the Spirit, as St Paul names it, may be ours even though we have no sensible, 'felt' experience of it. 'That which is born of the flesh is flesh, and that which is born of the Spirit is spirit,' and is spiritually discerned, not sensibly, save as God wills. The stirring of the emotions in worship and prayer may be due to something very far from the activity of the Spirit of God. Spiritual joy is the consequence of a generous, giving love of the divine lover. 'If you only knew,' writes St Thérèse, 'how great is my joy in giving pleasure to Jesus by the acceptance of the deprivation of all joy . . . this is the very refinement of joy – the joy we do not even feel.'

So in Lent we are to await holy Easter with spiritual joy and desire. One of the greatest hindrances to progress in the Christian life is our absorption in, and desire to be filled and satisfied with, the things along the way, instead of seeing and using them as means to an end which lies beyond. Like foolish children we want both to eat our cake and have it; we look to the things of religion to quench our hunger and thirst when in truth they are intended to excite and increase it. For whilst they lead us to, they do not give us what alone can satisfy us – God himself.

First Sunday in Lent

The practices of Lent

Let us now look at the particular means which St Benedict would have us place foremost in our Lenten observance.

They are prayer with tears, holy reading, compunction of heart, abstinence and self-denial in food, drink, sleep, talking and laughter.

First the giving of ourselves to prayer, for, as the saint says earlier in the Rule, 'Whatever good work you begin to do, beg of God with most earnest prayer to perfect it'. For as the inspiration to do good comes from God, and not from ourselves, so also can that good be carried out and perfected by the aid of his grace. The prayers of the church constantly remind us of this, as, for example, on the First Sunday after Trinity, 'because through the weakness of our mortal nature we can do no good thing without thee, grant us the help of thy grace', which truth is reiterated on the Ninth Sunday, and on the Second Sunday of Lent in the collect of which we confess that 'we have no power of ourselves to help ourselves'.

We are to 'give ourselves' to prayer, for it is a work which demands the whole of our being, the attention and employment of every faculty. We often complain of the difficulty of prayer, as if this were something to cause surprise. But what real work is not difficult, demanding, calling for the best in us? And prayer is a work, not a pastime, in which energy and perseverance must be joined to desire. To pray well is a gift of God which will not fail him who seeks it but it must be sought, and will be developed only by constant practice.

To pray with tears need not be interpreted literally, for tears, as both psychology and history will teach us, are a matter of temperament and custom. Today we are rather ashamed of tears but it is not so long ago that our forefathers (Nelson, for example) gave way to them quite naturally, as did Christians of earlier ages. And there is a set of beautiful prayers in the Missal in which we pray that God will 'draw out of our stony hearts the tears of repentance', such as shall 'quench the burning flames we most justly deserve and wash away the defilements of our sins'. David's *Miserere* contains the substance, and expresses the inmost meaning of St Benedict's 'prayer with tears'.

'Holy reading.' An idea of what is meant by this is given in chapter forty-seven of the Rule where we find it referred to, and legislated for, under the terms *lectio divina*, 'sacred reading', and, more simply, *lectio*, 'reading', for which a considerable time is allotted. Such reading was largely devoted to holy Scripture, and especially, no doubt, to those portions not included in the lessons at Matins. But it also included sacred study as well as more definitely 'spiritual' books such as the *Conferences of Cassian* and the Lives of the Fathers. But in Lent a special book is to be given to each monk from the library, 'to be read through carefully'.

It is more necessary than ever nowadays to emphasise the place of spiritual reading, especially as an aid to mental prayer for which it supplies the material. But we shall do well to choose and stick to one book, in addition of course to the Bible, and to read and reread it carefully, and, even more important, think about what we read. Many of the saints made a constant companion of one book for several years, as St Francis de Sales did the *Spiritual Combat* of Scupoli, thoroughly digesting and putting its teaching into practice. The multiplication of books in our day too often tempts people to read without much thought, and so to pass from one book to another, having gained little or nothing from any of them. Our Lent book should be one which aids our Lenten task, and 'spiritual' in character, but those who have time and opportunity may well give themselves to some study of any subject of a serious nature about which they ought, or may well, be informed. The general ignorance of 'pious' persons, not least amongst the so-called 'educated' class of the community, is astounding and deplorable.

'Compunction of heart'. For 'a broken heart, O God, Thou wilt not despise'. Compunction means to be pierced with something, and in Lent what is this but heartfelt sorrow for our sins, and also a tender compassion with the sorrow of the pierced heart of Jesus? It is not David's compunction alone, but our Lady Mary's, through whose soul pierced the sharp sword of sorrow as beneath the cross she became one with the passion of her son.

'Abstinence'. Since in the next paragraph St Benedict speaks of bodily abstinence, it may well be that he uses the term here in a more general sense. And indeed, necessary as the former may be, abstinence with regard to mind, imagination, memory, and emotions is much more important. It is of little use to abstain from food, etc., if these faculties are not brought under control, and kept from squandering themselves on all kinds of vain and useless matters, and in mere emotionalism. From how many thoughts and imaginations, how many sinful memories, how much daydreaming, we need to abstain! How great our need to control our emotions, learning to live and act by reason and faith rather than by impulses and feelings! How much, too, we need to abstain from certain things which, to any one in particular, may become occasions of sinful thoughts and imaginations, revive memories which should be forgotten, or stir emotions to our harm!

'Denying the body somewhat of food, drink, and sleep, talking and laughter'. In what this 'somewhat' is to consist, and in what measure, must be determined by each one both in the spirit of generosity which has been spoken of and in that of the prudence and discretion which is a marked characteristic of our saint's teaching. The English words 'talking and laughter' hardly convey the sense of his *loquacitas* and *scurrilitas* which would be better translated 'talkativeness of a vain, useless nature' (our Lord's 'idle words'), and 'foolish, excessive, vulgar and contemptuous laughter'. 'A man's excessive laughter shows what he is', says the book of Proverbs, and 'a fool lifteth up his voice with laughter'.

Monday of the First Week in Lent

The nature and character of the Holy Rule

Before we pass to the consideration of the fundamental truths and principles upon which the Holy Rule rests, and which govern all its prescriptions, we may note something of its nature, character and intention.

It is quite obviously written for the ordinary person, for any one of the multitudes such as listened to our Lord and from which he chose his apostles; the wayward, sinning, falling, and rising people in any and every state of life who, despite all their inconstancy and failures, desire to know, love, and serve God. We are apt to think of those who enter the religious life as being of a particularly pious nature and disposition, but it is clear from many parts of the Rule, and no less from the history of religious orders, that St Benedict and his successors had no such illusions. Many aspirants to the religious life were of noble family, educated, cultured, and pious; many were from the ranks illiterate and pious; others, not a few, were a rough, not particularly pious lot who needed severe discipline, much training and even corporal punishment to keep them in order. The Rule requires the abbot to 'manifest the sternness of a master and the loving affection of a father'. It envisages the presence in the monastery of the undisciplined and restless, the stubborn and negligent, the hardhearted, proud and disobedient, the lazy who do not rise promptly in the morning, murmurers, those who are slothful in study, given to idleness and foolish talking, or to 'the vice of hoarding'.

Additional evidence as to the kind of people who might be found in any monastery is given in the chapter on

The Instruments of Good Works in which, as we shall see later, not only is there nothing, except the duty of obedience to the abbot, which is not applicable to every Christian, but also many of the good works mentioned are such as we should hardly expect to find in a Rule for religious. Yet what is a religious but a Christian fulfilling his life in a particular vocation, one who will certainly not be a good religious save by being first a good Christian. But it is not necessarily as a good Christian, but only as one who desires to be one, that he comes to the monastery which, St Benedict will tell him, is 'a school of the Lord's service', for which he has written 'this little rule for beginners' who by 'observing it in monasteries may show that in some measure they have goodness of manners, and a beginning of religious life'.

The Holy Rule, then, lays a foundation, characterised, as every foundation ought to be, by simplicity, strength, and order. With the Apostle, St Benedict could say, 'According to the grace of God given to me, like a skilled master builder I laid a foundation . . . Each builder must choose with care how to build on it.'[1] Here is no shifting sand but solid rock upon which we may build with assurance and safety, for it is, in Bossuet's words, an epitome of Christianity, a learned abridgement of all the doctrines of the Gospel, all the institutions of the Fathers, and all the Counsels of Perfection.

The need of such a foundation for every Christian life is one of those things which is so obvious that there is danger of our forgetting it. When we are looking at and admiring a great and beautiful building, it is rarely that we think of the hidden foundation upon which it is raised, and to which those responsible for the preservation of the building must give attention. And this is the more necessary in the case of a great building which, erected in what were once quiet and undisturbed surroundings, is now subject to all the stress and strain of modern traffic. It is useless to keep an eye on walls and pillars if the foundations are neglected. This is no less true of that spiritual house, that 'palace which is not for human beings but for the Lord God'. The strength, the stability and the very beauty of that house depend upon the character of the foundation, the sureness by which it is laid, and the slow, patient, persevering care with which the materials are used and bound together in one unshakeable, indestructible whole.

Yet there would seem to be not a few Christians who are more concerned with adding to and decorating their souls than with giving constant and growing attention to the foundations. A multiplicity of devotions and practices, a feverish interest in the externals of divine worship, often dictated more by sentimental rather than by rational considerations, by nature rather than by grace, usurps the place which ought to be held by the great truths of the faith, and the Christian virtues which are, as the term implies, the true strength of the soul.

It must be seen that the one purpose of all the things of religion is to bind the soul to God, and to that end all must be used to forward that seeking 'truly after God' which St Benedict names as the one aim of the religious life. But not of the monk, friar, or nun alone, but of each baptised person whatever his or her vocation may be. Unless God is sought first, all else is useless. The Christian life must be a continual return to God, a drawing nearer to him, a constant increase in virtues of faith, hope and charity by which alone we are united to him. And this means much more attention to God himself than is often given. For the knowledge of God (not merely knowledge *about* God, necessary as this is) is eternal life, the life of union with God, our salvation and sanctification, the foundation upon which our house shall stand securely and eternally when all that is temporal, and all the means by which it has been built up, have passed away, and nought remains but God himself and that which, by his grace, we have become: living stones in the temple of his glory.

Tuesday of the First Week in Lent

The school of Jesus Christ

The Holy Rule lays a foundation; it is for beginners, and it is marked by a grave, discreet, moderate and practical simplicity. St Benedict states his intention 'to establish a school of the Lord's service, in the institution of which we hope to order nothing harsh or rigorous'. If, as he continues, 'anything be somewhat strictly laid down, according to the dictates of equity', it is only 'for the amendment of vices, or the preservation of charity'.

St Benedict's school is but one department of the much wider school of Jesus Christ who invites all people to come and learn of him, the Master of eternal truth, himself the very truth he would have us know and love. To this school we are to come as children, disciples, hearers and learners, not as self-opinionated adults, critics, or cavillers. Like St Ignatius of Loyola, who at the age of thirty-three sat on a low bench with schoolboys in order to learn Latin in preparation for the courses in philosophy and theology, to which he devoted some eleven years of his life, we must come with humility, docility and the desire to learn what no human wisdom can teach us, and to unlearn much that we have learnt in the world's school. Whatever other knowledge we may possess entitles us to no advanced form in this school; we must begin at the beginning, and that with a frank and entire surrender to the divine Master, to whom with St Peter we cry, 'Lord, to whom can we go? You have the words of eternal life.'[2]

Our Lord has given many leaders to his church since that day when he commanded his apostles to 'Go, and teach all nations',[3] having assured them that 'he who heareth you, heareth me'.[4] And not least among them is the saint at whose feet thousands of disciples have sat throughout the ages, as we do this Lent, and heard his opening words, 'Hearken, O my son, to the precepts of your master, and incline the ear of your heart; willingly receive and faithfully fulfil the admonition of your loving father'. An effort, an attention, an endeavour on our part is necessary. We are to come not simply to listen, as Tennyson's *Northern Farmer* to the preacher,

> a bummin' awaay loike a buzzard-clock ower my 'ead,
> An' I niver knaw'd whot a mean'd, but I thowt a'ad summut to saay,

but 'to hearken' . . . to incline our inward ear, to receive the essence of the spoken word into our minds, to take it in, apprehend and make it our own. How far has this been so in the past? Of all our hearing of the word of God, how much have we truly heard, received, assimilated, translated into life and conduct? The divine seed has not been wanting, but what of the soil? What barren or weed-covered fields are these upon which the heavenly Sower gazes? What have we done with the word of God?

'Hearken'. We do not hear with our ears, but with our minds. If while we are listening to a piece of music a train of thought about something else enters our mind, we no longer hear the music; for what is in the mind drowns what comes to the ear. We speak of people shutting their ears to the truth; but it is the mind alone to which truth is addressed, and which can receive or reject it. We may be compelled to listen with our ears, but there is no power which can compel our minds. Here we are free, a choice must be made as to what we will to hear. 'Incline the ear of your heart', that is, of your desire, and, as the saint adds later, open your eyes, the eyes of your mind, 'to the deifying light', that you may 'hear with wondering ears what the divine voice admonishes us, daily crying out, "Today if ye shall hear his voice, harden not your hearts." And again, "He that hath ears to hear, let him hear what the Spirit saith to the churches." And what says he? "Come, My children, hearken unto me, I will teach you the fear of the Lord."' 'Receive and faith fulfil.' The word received is a source of, and incentive to, action. The seed sown must find in the soil that which stirs it to life, fulfils it, or it will decay and die. There is no magic about the word of God; powerful as it is, it awaits our full co-operation to produce its fruit.

The first purpose of the divine word is, 'That you may return by the labour of obedience to him from whom you departed by the sloth of disobedience'. St Benedict does not hide the fact that what is required of us is not easy, it is a labour. For to return is more difficult than to begin, or to go straight on.

When one has taken a wrong turning, there is the temptation to go on in the hope that all will be well in the end. To go back is to admit our mistake, perchance our folly and obstinacy in not listening to advice given, to face a certain weariness in retracing our steps on a path which has simply to be got over before we strike the right way again. And how true this is of a change of mind, the surrender of accustomed opinions and ways of thought which have led us into ruts from which it is difficult to escape. No word of Jesus Christ was more demanding than that with which he began his mission, 'Change your minds'.

But there is only one way home, and it is well that we should return to it ere the night shadows fall, or before we have gone so far on our own way that we have lost the desire to return. There is a voice calling to us, but the further we go on the less capable we become of hearing it. 'Today if you will hear his voice, harden not your hearts.'[5] The mind hardens first, becomes set dulled with false imagination, not perceiving what it would see, were it less fanciful. The will weakens, loses its energy, becomes crippled and halting. Slowly but inevitably the heart centres on self, desire for God shrinks and dies, the door swings to and is closed. There is One who knocks without – but is not heard.

The sloth of disobedience

'The sloth of disobedience.' It is an unfamiliar and striking phrase. We are accustomed to think of disobedience as an activity, a revolt, a throwing off of binding chains, a sign of spirit. But St Benedict, to use a modern expression, 'debunks' it, calls it by its true name, exposes it as a counterfeit, an impostor.

For disobedience is a refusal to respond to our duty as creatures, subjects, servants, soldiers, sons and daughters; a relapse into a denial of, or an indifference to, the fact and the rights of God. It is to fail to take our rightful place, to do our part; to stand aloof and idle, we who are 'of the multitude of the Lord's workers'; to refuse to traffic with the goods committed to us. 'You wicked, lazy servant!'[6] It is to make a claim which has nothing to support it, and which we are unable to implement, the claim to independence and self-sufficiency. The sloth of disobedience is the first step by which life falls into confusion, disintegrates, becomes meaningless. The disobedient are as people who sit down by the wayside and fall into a sleep, the uneasy dreams of which they mistake for a real, waking activity.

To such is the call to return to God by the labour of obedience addressed 'whoever you are', says the saint, for 'God will have all [people] to be saved', and come to the knowledge of the truth. Despite the very prevalent idea of many English people, the Christian religion is not a rather close preserve for nice or more piously inclined people with a certain amount of leisure. Such an idea – unknown in Catholic countries – as any observant traveller may note, is largely due, not only to the Protestant and Puritan tendency to exalt respectability into a Christian virtue, and to regard poverty as a crime, or a punishment inflicted by God upon sin, but also to the emphasis laid upon *doing* rather than upon *being*, upon 'religious' practices more than upon the living out of the Christian life in the world. Practices are necessary, but the church makes very few of obligation, well knowing that the majority of her children have neither time nor capacity for more. The modern – but dying – cult of 'church going' which has so superseded both frequent attendance at Mass and the use of churches for private prayer, has little to recommend it except to those who have too much spare time on their hands. A greater realisation is needed of the fact that the salvation and sanctification of souls is wrought out, not merely within the walls of a church, but in the common ways of daily life. St Benedict makes the Christian life revolve round, and be expressed in, three activities, worship, work and study, and he had no sympathy with those who exalted one of these at the expense of another. For each must have its place in a truly balanced, Christian life.

And each demands a labour of obedience. Each is an activity which calls for the best in, and the whole of our being. To worship is not to sit or kneel listening to or watching what some one else is doing, be it priest or choir. Churches are not concert halls or lecture rooms, they are 'places of worship', and that worship must be our own, not somebody else's. It is both an act and an attitude; an act requiring our full co-operation and attention, and an attitude which, cultivated in the direct act of approach to God, flows out into, and determines, every other activity of our normal lives. For it is not merely the act performed in church, but also the abiding attitude of our lives which is our worship. 'Whatever you do, in word or deed, do everything in the name of the Lord Jesus',[7] that is in the person, and with the mind of him who is the one worshipper, in whom alone the Father may be worshipped 'in spirit and in truth'.

We need not, then, expect worship to be easy, especially if

by the sloth of disobedience we have neglected it, or drifted into a formal, perfunctory habit of thought and attention when at worship. To return to a worship which is a real giving of ourselves to God, in union with the giving of our Lord, involves the labour of obedience, since only one who renders obedience in all things to him may offer a worship acceptable in his sight. Slothfulness in worship is a reflection of slothfulness in life, the failure to recognise what is owing to God, and to pay what is justly due to him.

All disobedience is the giving to another of what ought to be given to God, the act of a quisling who renders to an usurper what is owing to his rightful sovereign. Nor is it, as is so often dreamed, the gaining of freedom, but the loss of it, the falling into a servitude, the imperious demands of which grow stronger every day. 'Know ye not, that to whom ye yield yourselves servants to obey, his servants ye are', whether of God or devil. No one is free in the absolute sense of the term, but is created a servant who may become free only in the service of God, in which, as a Collect says, 'is perfect freedom', 'the glorious freedom of the children of God'.[8] In this service we grow, expand, become our true selves, fulfil the purpose of our being; in any other we become less than we might be, 'deformed', incapable of realising the capacities of our God-given nature, still less of rising from the place of a servant to that of the freeman and friend of God.

It may be a labour to return from the sloth of disobedience to the service of God, since we have so weakened ourselves in a service which could give us nothing in return. But love's labour is never lost, nor indeed hard, compared with the driving, useless slavery of sin, and St Benedict will tell us how it may be begun and accomplished. 'Whatever good work you begin to do, beg with most earnest prayer to God that he will perfect it . . . asking him to supply by his grace what by nature is hardly possible to us'.

The fact of God

We have spoken of the Holy Rule as laying a foundation, and before we consider the implications of this fact, we must see what are the fundamental truths and principles upon which it is based, and which actuate and determine all that St Benedict teaches.

It would be impossible to read the Rule carefully without seeing how the saint is impressed with the fact, the majesty, and the presence of God. We have the sense of listening to one who stands in the authentic line of the patriarchs and prophets, one whose every word expresses that deep awe and reverence with which God should be approached and spoken of. It is this which sets upon the Rule a certain simplicity and austerity which, however differing from that of the Fathers of the desert in practice, yet breathes their spirit, and has ever been a characteristic mark of Benedictine life and piety.

God is – this is the supreme fact which all people must face and reckon with. Beyond all the things of the finite and temporal order, before all things and all time, the infinite and eternal Being, supreme Spirit, not merely above but different from all created beings, God is the *I Am That I Am.* His transcendent, all-powerful majesty, before which the angelic hierarchy veil their faces in profoundest adoration, is the fount and source from which springs all created being and life. His presence fills all things, both causing and sustaining them in their appointed order. His eyes behold the whole universe, and the most secret thoughts of people, in one comprehensive, all-knowing glance. All authority, dominion, and power devolve from him and must be accounted for to him.

Upon this one supreme fact of the being and existence of God rests our whole relation to him. There can be no equality between humanity and God, no question of the rights of individuals as against the sovereignty of God, no arrangements or compromises between the creature and the Creator. There can be a covenant, a pact between God and humanity, but it is God who makes it, not a round-table conference of people with, as it were, God in the chair. The peace of God is dictated to the rebels who, in St Benedict's words, 'renounce their own wills, and take up the strong and bright weapons of obedience' in order that henceforth 'They may fight for Christ, their true King'.

We are indebted to God for all that we are and have; God owes nothing to us as of right, nor needs anything from us. What he bestows upon us he does, not of necessity, but of love and mercy; what he demands of us is not for his own gain, but for ours. Humanity comes from God, belongs to God, is all-dependent upon God, and this involves obligations, duties, responsibilities on our part. To fear God, to worship, love, reverence, obey, and serve him, this is for us to stand in our place, fulfil the purpose of our being, and in so doing to realise our perfection in becoming what God created us to be.

It is true that since a measure of freedom, a capacity of choice, has been conferred upon us, we cannot be compelled to fulfil our obligations. For God is just, and treats each of his creatures according to the nature which he has given them.

Since, also, as we have said, the obligations which are inherent in the relationship of the creature to the Creator are for humanity's benefit, not for God's, it is humanity that gains by fulfilling them, or suffers for the neglect of them. We may defy God, refuse him service, withhold our love and obedience, but in so doing we but harm ourselves. Each blow aimed at God returns upon the one who aims it, each neglect lessens, and detracts from, whoever is guilty of it.

The fact that God is entails other facts about the existence and nature of which St Benedict has no illusions. Judgement, heaven, and hell are as factual and inescapable as is the fact of God. With the stark realism of holy Scripture, the Holy Rule speaks of God not only as a loving but as an 'angry Father . . . a dread Lord, incensed by our sins'; of the 'dreadful judgement of God' which is to be feared, and before which every person must render an account; of 'the pain of hell' wherein 'those who despise God will be consumed for their sins'.

We shall see that this is not the whole of the story, but it is an integral part which may not be omitted or obscured. St Benedict is not dealing with opinions or pious fancies, but with facts more real and enduring than those of the temporal order, facts which, however much we may interpret them in a more spiritual manner than did people of the sixth century, are not lessened but indeed made more terribly significant. Whether the 'fire' of hell is of a material nature or not is immaterial in view of the fact that hell does consist in the knowledge that God, and all truth and goodness, beauty and freedom, all that makes for life, has been lost by one's own fault, and that the self has become hate and misery instead of love and delight.

St Benedict will have much to say of the love and mercy of God, of the grace of Christ, and the joy of heaven. But, unlike many modern teachers, he does not omit the foundations, nor minimise the truths upon which alone a right understanding and appreciation of the love and mercy of God can rest. The New Testament revelation is incomparably greater than that of the Old Testament which it assumes, builds upon and fulfils. But it is no less plain and severe, and in proclaiming that 'God is love' leaves us in no doubt that the rejection of such love, the neglect of such mercy, makes a soul unfit for the seen, known, loved presence of God, from which, however, it cannot escape. And this is its hell.

Friday of the First Week in Lent

The fact a fact to us

God is. We do well not to take this fact too much for granted, or hurry away from the consideration of its meaning and implications. For we need not merely to believe in the fact of God' s existence, but to be impressed by it, to let it sink into our minds and hearts, until it becomes a living, potent, moving power in our lives. For like so many lesser but very real facts, there is a danger of our accepting it without any, or much, realisation of its tremendous import. Its very familiarity, even if it does not breed contempt, may cause a certain attitude such as we come to adopt with regard to great and known facts which have yet not affected us personally.

We have known, for example, of the existence of the horrors of war all our lives, and have expressed our concern about them. But what was this so long as they did not touch us? Not until we lost someone who was dear to us, or the bombs fell upon our cities, did we really begin to know what war means. So is it with the fact of God. It must come near to us, touch us, impress us, before it can become actually real to us. Or rather, since God is ever near to us, even when unthought of and unperceived, we must come near to him. Our minds must be 'set on things above', not 'above' in the sense of spatially far away, but above the things of earth and the consideration of merely human things. Of a certain young man it was said that 'he had been brought up to believe in God but not to think about him'. It is a common fault, as disastrous as it is common, for only what we think about becomes real to us, enters into us, influences us.

But is not the important thing to love God? Yes, but who can love what they have not bestowed some thought upon;

or who do not think of the ones whom they love? And men and women do not, at least normally, 'fall in love' with God; indeed, many will tell you that they see no reason why they should. 'See no reason', that is the reason. 'We needs must love the highest when we see it,' wrote the poet; but who will love what they do not see? And how many there are whose minds are blinded by the god of this world, 'to keep them from seeing the light of the gospel of the glory of Christ, who is the image of God'![9] If we do not have God in our thoughts we are little likely to have him in our hearts.

To most of us God comes as one of whom we have heard, but who is virtually a stranger. He knocks at our door, presents letters of introduction, is received with a certain courtesy on our part, and in time becomes desired as a friend or disliked as a bore. For we cannot but become conscious that his very kindness and courtesy is making demands upon us, that he is claiming our time and attention, quietly refusing to be left alone or treated cursorily, until we begin to feel that our house is no longer our own. We cannot complain that he has behaved badly, nor point to anything in which he has been wrong. But in a manner beyond our understanding he is for ever making his presence felt, is exercising an attraction to which we feel we must surrender, or from which we must escape. The former is not easy; the latter we shall discover is impossible, if we attempt it. We cannot turn him out, we can only try and ignore him, go our own way as if he were not. Yet there is no change in him, but all else has changed. We are like Francis Bernardone on that day when, pursued by the divine Lover, he gazed upon the beauty of the Vale of Spoleto, and for the first time found no joy in it. Things have turned against us who turned from him whose they are

> Lo, all things fly thee, for thou fliest me!
> Strange, piteous, futile thing,
> Wherefore should any set thee love apart?

Everything grasped at apart from God, or before God, crumbles, passes, slips through our fingers, until we are left alone. No – not alone, for God remains, 'waiting daily,' says St Benedict, 'for us to respond by our deeds to his holy admonitions.' Therefore are the days of our life lengthened for the amendment of our evil ways, as says the apostle, 'Knowest thou not that the patience of God leadeth thee to repentance?'

We shall do well, whoever we are, to let our mind dwell upon that fact of God, patiently waiting for our eyes to turn towards him, as once he hung patiently upon the cross our sins had prepared for him. It is for this that 'the days of our life are lengthened', for this that we are still living in time and surrounded by opportunities of 'amending our evil ways'. Each day is a revelation of 'the patience of God' which would draw us to himself. That patience is indeed infinite and inexhaustible but the days of our lives are numbered and quickly pass, never to return. We have so much time, no more, and how much we do not know. Time is not in our hands, but in God's. 'My time is in thy hand, O God.' 'So teach us to number our days,' to take account of and make use of them, 'that we may apply our hearts unto wisdom.' For, says the book of Proverbs, they who regarded not wisdom 'gat not only this hurt, that they knew not the things which were good; but also left behind them to the world a memorial of their foolishness . . . but wisdom delivered from pain those that attended upon her . . . for she is a treasure that never fails: which they that use become the friends of God.' And why is this? Because the wise know how to order life aright in relation not only to the things of this world, and this is important, but also toward God, and the things of eternity. They see the true value of time and set themselves, in St Peter's words, to redeem it; they are alive to the opportunities and graces which come their way, hasten 'to do now what will profit [them] for eternity . . . while there is yet time, while [they are] still in the flesh and able to fulfil all these things by which the light is given'. For they know that 'night is coming when no one can work'.[10]

The presence of God

'We believe that the divine presence is everywhere, and that the eyes of the Lord behold the good and evil in every place.' (Chapter xix)

So St Benedict combines in one simple sentence two conceptions of the presence of God: the one of the divine immanence of him in whom 'we live and move and have our being',[11] the other of God in heaven embracing in one eternal and all-knowing glance the thoughts, ways, and acts of all people. 'Thou, God, seest me,' is a dominant and recurring thought in the Holy Rule. In the chapter on Humility the saint bids his disciples 'consider that [they are] always beheld from heaven by God, and that their actions are everywhere seen by the eye of the divine Majesty, and are every hour reported to him by his angels', and again, 'In regard to the desires of the flesh, we must believe that God is ever present with us, as the prophet says to the Lord, "O Lord, all my desire is before Thee." . . . Since, therefore, the eyes of the Lord behold good and evil; and the Lord is ever looking down from heaven upon the [people of the world], to see who has understanding, or is seeking God; and since the works of our hands are reported to him, our maker and creator, day and night by the angels appointed to watch over us: we must be always on the watch . . . lest, as the prophet says in the psalm, God should see us at any time declining to evil and becoming unprofitable; and lest, though he spares us now, because he is merciful and waits for our conversion, he should say to us hereafter: "These things thou didst and I held my peace."'

It is as foolish as it is easy, and indeed common in many who ought to know better, to ridicule such scriptural language as 'anthropomorphic', or to regard it as implying that God is a merciless inquisitor who delights in keeping his children in a state of anxious fear, a bogey to frighten us into being good. As to the former, it is impossible for us to speak of the activity of the personal, living God save in the terms of our common speech which, whilst it expresses a truth, is yet capable of being misunderstood, since the things of the divine order of being cannot be fully expressed in human language, which can never be used of God and humanity in exactly the same sense. This is so whether we speak of God seeing all things, or of his presence in all things. For he does not see as we do, either with our eyes or our minds, nor is he present anywhere as we are present in a particular place. To say that God sees all things is to mean that he knows all things in one eternal act of knowledge, for he does not simply know things because they exist, as we do, but his knowledge is the cause of their existence.

So, too, when we speak of the presence of God we have to divest our minds of all notions of a physical, or material, presence of one who because he is present *here* cannot be present *there*. For 'God is Spirit'[12] and as such is present everywhere, not as being contained or limited by any thing or place, but as the Cause of all things, who by his all-pervading and ever-active power sustains and preserves all creation in being. Perhaps the nearest created thing we know to the presence of God is the invisible, intangible air which surrounds us, which is both without and within us an ever-present immense force always in action and upon which our physical life depends. So, in a much greater sense, does the divine presence envelop and sustain our being, as it does that of the whole universe, and this so completely and necessarily that if it were to cease all creation would relapse into the nothingness from which it sprang at the bidding of the Word 'by whom all things were made'.

The truth of the immanence of God, of his universal presence, in which all things live and move and have their being, must not be understood to mean that he is the sum total in all things, or, in other words, that the creator and his creation are one and the same. For it is his transcendence, his very 'otherness' to all creation, his being above, beyond, before, and different from creatures, which enables him to be in all things, or as it is more true to say, for all things to be in him, since the material cannot contain the spiritual in such a manner as it can something of its own nature.

God is not more present in any one place than in another, but he may be more differently or more powerfully present in one thing or place than in another. Thus his presence in humanity is quite different from that in the animal or plant, more powerful in the saint than in the sinner, since the latter, by the exercise of will, hinders God's expression of his presence. So, also, he may be more powerfully present in certain places wherein he chooses to make some special manifestation of himself.

The simple, elementary character of the truth that 'in God we live and move and have our being'[13] must not lead us to minimise its importance. We must reflect upon it that we may be impressed by it as was St Benedict, and be moved and influenced by it. For nothing can be more important than the fact that, wherever we are, whatever we are doing, at worship or at work, at prayer or at play, in the sanctuary or in the street, in seeking after God or sinning against him, we are living, moving, acting in and by the power of the divine presence from which not for one instant may we escape. Remembered or forgotten, acted upon or ignored, it matters not, for 'there is no creature that is not manifest in his sight: but all things are naked and open before the eyes of him with whom we have to do'.

It is not enough simply to believe this; 'the devils also believe and tremble'[14] whilst we are often indifferent and unconcerned. If the fact of the presence of God and his all-seeing knowledge, real as it is, is to become a reality to us, we must become familiar with it, think of it, wake up to it, get used to it as one gets used to living in new surroundings, or, better, as one suddenly begins to recognise and appreciate the value of things which lie around us. For, as says St Augustine, commenting on the words, 'Of him, and through him, and in him, are all things', all are not with him in that sense in which it is said to him, 'I am continually with thee'. Nor is he with all in that way in which we say, 'The Lord be with you'. And this is the especial wretchedness of humanity, not to be with him without whom we cannot live. For, without doubt, we cannot be separate from him in whom we exist; yet if we do not remember, know, and love him, we are not with him.

So many practices have become common since St Benedict's day that we are apt to forget that of the presence of God. Yet it may be questioned whether any practice is more necessary, or more calculated to advance our spiritual life, to be a constant safeguard against temptation, and a continual reinforcement and comfort amidst all the varying conditions and circumstances of our daily lives. 'I have set God always on my right hand, therefore shall I not fall.' Here is humility and confidence, dependence and courage, strong faith and sure hope, in which we may walk securely toward our goal.

SECOND SUNDAY IN LENT

The urgency of the call of God

That sense of the factual character of divine and eternal realities which pervades the Holy Rule gives to it a note of urgency, of the necessity of action, prompt, decisive, definite. 'Harken . . . incline the ear of your heart . . . let us then at length arise . . . run while you have the light of life, lest the darkness of death seize hold upon you . . . for we shall by no means reach the kingdom of God unless we run thither by our good deeds . . . if we would arrive at eternal life, escaping the pains of hell, then while there is yet time, while we are still in the flesh, and are able to fulfil all these things by the light which is given us – we must hasten to do now what will profit us for eternity.'

For, it is God who calls, the divine voice, 'daily crying out, "Today if ye will hear his voice, harden not your hearts."[15] And again, "He that hath ears to hear, let him hear."'[16] It is the Lord who 'is waiting daily for us to respond by our deeds to His holy admonitions. Therefore are the days of our life lengthened out for the amendment of our evil ways, as says the Apostle "Knowest thou not that the patience of God is leading thee to repentance?"'

It is the loving Father who 'has vouchsafed to count us in the number of his children' and invites us, 'Come, my children, hearken unto me. I will teach you the fear of the Lord'. It is the divine householder 'seeking his own workman in the multitude of the people, to whom he cries out, "Who is the man that will have life, and desires to see good days?" What can be sweeter to us than this voice of the Lord inviting us? Behold in his loving kindness the Lord shows unto us the way of life. Having our loins, therefore, girded with faith, and the performance of good works, let us walk in his paths by the guidance of the gospel that we may deserve to see him who has called us to his kingdom.'

There is nothing new in all this, but how much there is which, too often, we take for granted and do little about. Well then that, having read the saint's words, we should go back and meditate upon them, that thought may issue in action, faith in good works

An effort is required of us, and that not merely once but constantly repeated. 'Let us, then, at length arise.' We have overslept and are heavy, listless, disinclined to stir ourselves. But the day has already dawned, the hours are passing, the light now so bright will fade into darkness, there comes a night 'in which no one can work'.[17] Already we have wasted time and dissipated energy in lying in bed instead of getting up and about. Again, the voice cries, 'Arise, it is high time to awake out of sleep, to open our eyes to the deifying light, to hear with wondering ears what the divine voice admonishes us, daily crying out, "Today if ye will hear his voice"... while there is yet time.' How much time? 'While we are still in the flesh and are able' to walk in the light and 'to do now what will profit us for eternity.' Today, now, at this moment which is still ours, for who has promised us another day, a tomorrow, another moment of fleeting time?

St Benedict, with the church and holy Scripture, is seized with the supreme importance of the present moment, which a later writer, Père Caussade, does not hesitate to call a sacrament, 'the sacrament of the present moment'. And such indeed it is, for each moment brings with it some outward task or opportunity in which is contained the inward grace which is needed both to see and use it aright. And it is in the right and fullest use of the present moment that our salvation and sanctification lies, not merely in those spent in church, in pious exercises and the reception of sacraments. These are *means* of salvation; the work of salvation is – or is not – going on in each moment, at and in every task. If, aided by grace, we are not working out our own salvation as the clock ticks out the moments in which we go about our common duties, we are not doing it in church or upon our knees. Life is not a series of disconnected incidents, it is a continuously growing, developing thing to which each moment and each act contributes.

To each day, then, we are to wake up with a sense of its unique and swiftly passing value, 'my single day' as Pippa calls it in Browning's poem:

> God lends to leaven
> What were all earth else, with a feel of heaven
> Meeting it in her joyous spirit and resolve.
> Oh, Day, if I squander a wavelet of thee,
> A mite of my twelve hours' treasure,
> The least of the gazes or glances,
> (Be they grants thou art bound to or gives above measure)
> One of thy choices or one of thy chances,
> (Be they tasks God imposed thee, or freaks at thy pleasure)
> – My Day, if I squander such labour or leisure,
> Then shame fall on Asolo, mischief on me.

For, in Guardini's words, 'A day is a way; it needs direction; it is a work; demanding definite resolution. A day is your whole life – your whole life is as your day. A will, a direction, a clear countenance, looking toward God, all this each moment brings to us.'

To be such, each day must begin with God whose gift it is and to whom, before our minds are occupied with its duties, we pay our homage, praise, and thanks, and so with clear minds, resolute wills and grateful hearts go out to our day, Christianly, calmly, confidently, welcoming and seizing upon each sacrament of its moments, so that 'never departing from the guidance of our divine Master but persevering in his teaching we may deserve to be partakers in his heavenly kingdom' with those who 'serve him day and night in his temple'.

Monday of the Second Week in Lent

The fear of God

God is. Whether we believe it or not, give heed to it or not, makes no difference. We are in presence of a Fact, a Reality, unalterable and inescapable, in which we live and move and have our being, upon which everything depends. And if the first consequence of this fact is the urgent necessity of recognising and acknowledging it, the second is the arousing within us of that spirit and attitude of the fear of the Lord by which, says holy Scripture, 'people depart from evil', and set themselves to 'serve God in reverence and holy fear'. For it is the mark of the sinner that there is 'no fear of God before his eyes', and 'an evil thing', says God, 'that my fear is not in thee'.

St Benedict bids us hear the divine voice calling, 'Come, My children, harken unto me, I will teach you the fear of the Lord', so that, inspired by that fear, we may 'serve him with the good things he has given us', lest 'as an angry Father' he 'disinherit his children', and as 'a dread Lord incensed by our sins, deliver us to everlasting punishment, as most wicked servants who would not follow him to glory'. Among the instruments of good works we find 'To fear the day of judgement' and 'To be afraid of hell'. In the chapter on obedience he speaks of 'the swiftness of the fear of God' by which 'at the same instant the bidding of the master and the perfect work of the disciple are together more perfectly fulfilled', and marks as the first step on the ladder of humility the act by which people 'with the fear of God always before [their] eyes avoid all forgetfulness, being ever mindful of all that God hath commanded, and that those who despise God will be consumed in hell for their sins; and let [them] ever reflect that life everlasting is prepared for them that fear him'. He reminds us that 'the eyes of the Lord behold both good and evil, that the Lord is ever looking down from heaven upon the [people of the world], to see who has understanding or is seeking him', and that 'we need to be ever watchful lest we incline to evil, and become unprofitable servants, so that, although he spare us now, because he is merciful and waits for our conversion, he should say to us hereafter, "These things thou didst, and I held my peace."'

What is this fear of the Lord of which holy Scripture says that 'it is the beginning of wisdom . . . a strong confidence . . . a fountain of life . . . is honour and glory . . . the first step to be accepted of him . . . the beginning of his love . . . and that there is none above him that feareth the Lord . . . no evil shall happen unto him . . . he shall not fear nor be afraid . . . for blessed is the soul that feareth the Lord'? This fear which we are bidden to have, no less in the New than in the Old Testament?

It is the awe, the deep worshipful reverence, the lowly prostration of the creature before the majesty, the holiness, the greatness, the purity, the transcendent, incomprehensible Being of the creator, without which religion is cheapened, and our approach to God savours of impertinence. It is the remembrance that although God is our most loving and merciful Father, he is God, before whom the choirs of angels veil their faces, and whose favour must not be presumed upon; that he is the sovereign Lord who claims our obedience and makes it the essential witness of our love for him. It is this fear which not only makes us avoid all sin because it displeases him, but also dictates the manner in which he is to be loved, worshipped, and served. It preserves us from indifference, from forgetfulness, from slovenliness in worship and service, from taking liberties with God, from lack of generosity in our giving to him. It reminds us that heaven may be lost, that hell is a possibility not to be disregarded, of both our littleness and our sinfulness, the poverty of our good, the immense and constant need we have of God. How could we dream that we could do without it when of our Lord himself it is said, that in the days of his flesh 'he was heard in that he feared', that 'godly fear' which, in a later chapter of the Epistle to the Hebrews, is coupled with reverence, 'that we may serve God acceptably with reverence and godly fear: for our God is a consuming fire'?[18] First of the seven gifts of the Spirit which in all their fullness rested upon him, we see it manifested in his unvarying attention to his Father's business, his single devotion and obedience to the divine will, his constant prayer, his subjection to Mary and Joseph, his respect for the Jewish church, and for those who, however unworthy, held high office in it, in that lowliness and meekness with which he walked amongst people, in the exquisite tenderness with which he dealt with sinners. So to see it in him is to know it as very different from any servile or craven fear, filled with foreboding and anxiety. Rather is it the source of 'a strong confidence' which 'tendeth to life', of courage, for 'it shall be well with them who fear the Lord' knowing that his eye 'is upon them that fear him', that to them he extends his mercy and pity, gives meat to, and 'fulfils all the desire of them that fear him'.

Thus are we bidden to 'serve the Lord with fear and rejoice before him', for in such fear is not only 'the beginning of wisdom', but the initial step which brings to the soul that love which 'casts out fear',[19] that love of God for his own sake of which St Francis Xavier speaks:

My God, I love thee, not because
I hope for heaven thereby,
nor yet because who love thee not
are lost eternally.
Not with the hope of gaining aught,
not seeking a reward,
but as thyself hast loved me,
O ever-loving Lord!

The end for which we are created

St Benedict sees the Christian life (of which the monastic life is but one form, or design for living) as a journey, a work, a warfare, a discipleship, which requires the whole of our attention and energy and is to be undertaken in view of a definite end. It is that end which gives meaning, purpose, direction to our human lives, so that although it comes last in the order of time, and in fulfilment, it must come first in mind and intention. We must know what the end is, why and how it is to be sought, the means which must be used, the qualities necessary to bring our journey, our work, our warfare to its goal. For no one is likely to undertake such a journey, or indeed any journey, work, warfare, or discipleship, without seeing some clear and compelling reason why they should do so. It is largely for lack of such knowledge about the goal of Christian life and practice that so many either refuse to make the journey or, if they do, treat it as a promenade, or 'sit at ease in Zion', indulging themselves with the good things of religion instead of using them as aids on the way, tools for work, weapons of warfare, knowledge to be put into action. The question, 'Why should I do this?' is more important than 'How should I do it?'

The Christian life, together with all the means by which it is sustained and advanced, has but one end, which, however, may be stated in two forms. That end is God himself, seen, known, and loved by humanity. It is also the perfection of human nature finally attained by, and in, the sight of God. For the end does not merely consist in coming to God, but in becoming like God. So St Paul writes of our knowing God as we are known of him, and St John that 'we shall be like him, for we shall see him as he is'.[20] And the words of

Jesus, 'Be perfect, therefore, as your heavenly Father is perfect',[21] are taken up and reiterated throughout the New Testament. That likeness to God is not, of course, one of nature, for there is an unbridgeable gulf between the nature of the Creator and that of the creature. Our perfection is to be that of a human nature perfect in its manner as God is perfect in his, a perfection of which our nature is capable, yet which it cannot realise and bring to fruition without the aid of divine grace. 'But to all who received him, who believed in his name, he gave power to become children of God.'[22]

Any end which we set before ourselves, and pursue with purpose and energy, as of a thing to be desired, attained, or accomplished, sets its mark upon us, determines the means and measure of our activity, moulds our character. We become what we give ourselves to. This is why, in giving ourselves to any earthly end, a necessity of every human life, we must guard the measure of our giving, lest it come so to possess us that the true end for which we were created be forgotten or ignored. For however true and good an earthly end may be, nay, because of its very truth and goodness, it has the power to blind and enslave us. And good servants as they are, they make but bad masters whom it is difficult to escape from once they have been allowed to forget their place As servants they aid, strengthen, support us, add to our lives; but as masters they hinder, weaken, betray us, and cause us to become less than we were created to be.

Far other is it when we give ourselves to God as our Final and Perfecting End. In this giving there can be no measure, as there is no loss. 'The measure of loving God is to love him without measure,' says St Bernard.

In this giving all is gain –
we lose what on ourselves we spend,
we have as treasure without end
whatever, Lord, to Thee we lend,
who givest all.

St Benedict constantly reminds us of the end to which everything in the Holy Rule is designed to bring us. He would have us listen to him in order that we may 'return to' God, 'truly seek him', 'deserve to see him', 'arrive at eternal life', 'gain from the Lord that reward which God himself has promised', 'hasten . . . to the height of perfection', and 'by a straight course reach our creator'.

It is an end outside and beyond time; above all the things of this world; an end unattainable by human nature in itself, since it exceeds our natural powers. But, no less, an end which is attainable by those who desire it, who seek for it, who use the means which God has provided; an end which cannot be lost save by one's own fault. However impossible it may be for us to imagine what it is like, we need have no doubt about the fact of it, for it is not merely something, it is God himself, to come to whom is to come to the creative source of all good, the fulfilment of every desire, the perfection of all delight, who created us for himself and has promised that we should share in his happiness and beatitude, and, having done all that even he could do for us, unceasingly calls us to come to him. 'What can be sweeter to us, dearest brethren,' asks St Benedict, 'than this voice of the Lord inviting us? Behold, in his loving kindness the Lord shows unto us the way of life.' And following in that way we may cry with St John of the Cross, even in the midst of earth's shadows, 'If I go, my God, whithersoever thou goest it will go with me as I desire for thy sake.'

Wednesday of the Second Week in Lent

The vision of God

'That we may deserve to see him who has called us into his kingdom.'

To see God – it is this vision for which the devout Jew, the pagan philosopher and the faithful Christian have looked, sought, and lived. In fact, wherever people have believed in God, there we find the deep conviction that the final, perfecting end of our being is to be found in the sight of him in whose image and likeness we are created. Philo of Alexandria, writing a little before the Beloved Disciple who said, 'We shall be like him, for we all see him as he is',[23] speaks of that holy warfare which a person would not leave 'until [they reap] the prize of victory. And what crown could be more fresh and welcome to the victorious soul than to see him who is with clear sight? It is a worthy conflict which awaits the ascetic soul, to win eyes for the clear vision of him whom alone it is worth man's while to see.' Maximus of Tyre tells of the soul's search for God under the guidance of pure reason and strong love, and says, 'As we draw near to heaven and leave earth behind, the goal shines with clear and luminous light, a foretaste of God himself. On the road we learn his nature – but when we reach the end, we shall see him,' and the seal of truth was set upon such hopes when Christ, the Light enlightening everyone coming into the world, not only proclaimed, 'Blessed are the pure in heart, for they shall see God,'[24] but also revealed himself as the way, the truth, and the life by which we should come to that vision.

But what are we to understand by 'seeing God'? And by what means may we arrive at that sight?

In the full sense of the word, God can be seen only after

this present life, and then by the purified mind in which indeed is all our true seeing. For to see God is to know him 'even as we are known',[25] as says the apostle. We are familiar with this use of the verb 'to see' as meaning 'to know' or 'to understand' as when we say, 'I see what you are driving at.' God cannot be seen with our eyes, since their capacity of vision is limited to the material, and 'God is Spirit', that is, immaterial. By the mind alone can God be seen, and this because it is immaterial, a spiritual faculty capable of apprehending and knowing the essence of things, and not merely their outward appearance. Yet to know God, as distinct from knowing that he is, the mind needs the supernatural illumination of faith here on earth, and an even greater assistance, the light of glory, in heaven.

God cannot be seen directly and immediately in this life, but only indirectly 'as in a mirror',[26] in his works, and, above all, in his Son, 'the express image of his Person'[27]. 'The heavens declare the glory of God,'[28] sings the psalmist, and the book of Proverbs, 'By the greatness and beauty of the creatures proportionately the Maker of them is seen.' The manifold variety of created things reflects in multitudinous forms that divine fullness and perfection which cannot be seen as a whole, but only as broken up and reflected in the mirror of his works. 'The invisible things of him from the creation of the world are clearly seen, being understood by the things which are made, even his eternal power and Godhead.'

But even this seeing of God is possible only to those who seek purity of heart and the single eye. Neither truth nor beauty forces itself upon us, 'truth makes eyes at no one,' says Bernanos. They demand an inward receptivity and response, he alone –

who looks aright
Can never want some image of His grace.

But the fullest and clearest sight of God possible on earth is that which faith enables us to see in the person of Jesus Christ. 'Whoever has seen me has seen the Father',[29] not in person for the Son is not the Father, but in act. 'If you know me, you will know my Father also. From now on you do know him and have seen him,'[30] for to know the true, express image is to know the original from whom the image is derived. For the Son is 'the brightness' of the glory of the Father, and in this brightness, writes Ruysbroeck, 'the Father knows himself and all that lives in him; for all that he has, and all that he is, he gives to the Son, save only the property of Fatherhood, which abides in himself. And this is why all that lives in the Father, unmanifested in the Unity, is also in the Son actively poured forth into manifestation,' and in him the hiddenness of God is revealed.

The full, unhindered vision of God is reserved for heaven, where the light of glory succeeds to that of faith, enabling the blessed to see God 'face to face'. In this vision, says Aquinas, the blessed possess three things: they see God, and in seeing him they possess him as present; having the power to see him always; and possessing him, they enjoy him 'as the ultimate fulfilment of every desire'. According to the word of the Psalmist, 'He fulfilleth the desire of all things living.' So does humanity attain to the perfection it is bidden to seek and become, for 'we shall be like him, for we shall see him as he is',[31] in that vision wherein –

> The Good, which is volition's goal,
> all gathers there, and the deficient rest
> outside it, there becomes a perfect whole.

Such is the end of which Jesus is the way, the truth, and the life, without whom we should not have the

> hardihood to dare
> The vision of the Goodness infinite.

and may well, with Dante, praise that –

> plenteous grace, whence I presumed to bear
> the stress of the eternal Light, till thirst
> was consummated in the seeing there!

Renouncing our own will

'To you, therefore, my words are now addressed, whoever you are, that, renouncing your own will, you do take up the strong and bright weapons of obedience, in order to fight for the Lord Christ, our true King.'

Having seen the end, the purpose for which we were created, and to fulfil which God has mercifully redeemed us and saved us by his grace, providing in his church all the means by which we are enabled to work out our own salvation, we now listen to St Benedict as he puts before us the way of salvation.

The first, and continually necessary step, is the renunciation of our own will, not, of course, the renunciation of the activity of the will, which is more than ever needed, but of its slavery to self-interest, our own will, as opposed to God's will for us. We have placed ourselves in the hands of a master to whom we owe docility and obedience, and the more complete this is, the more we shall discover the truth of the phrase, 'Whose service is perfect freedom'.

The expression 'free will' is misleading, not only because a will which was not free would not be a will at all, but also because no will, save that of God, is altogether free. What human wills possess is the capacity to attain freedom, and this they can do, not by self-will, but only by accomplishing God's will. So the Schoolmen[32] preferred the term 'free choice', for here is the crux of the whole matter, since it is by its choices that the will gains or loses its freedom.

To renounce one's own will means nothing less than that renunciation of self, of which our Lord has spoken so plainly, 'If any want to become my followers, let them deny themselves and take up their cross and follow me.'[33] For the will is not a faculty which is exercised independently of the rest of our being. It is our whole self directed toward a particular end. It is what we are in action.

St Augustine, in his *Confessions*, tells how, on the eve of his conversion, he sat in the garden of his lodgings in Milan, unable to make up his mind whether to become a Catholic or not. He could see that the one thing necessary was 'to will to go, to will resolutely and thoroughly; not to turn and toss, this way and that, a maimed and divided will, struggling, with one part sinking as another rose'. He was astonished to find how easily and immediately his body obeyed his will, whilst his mind so resisted it. 'Whence is this monstrous thing,' he asks, 'that the mind commands the body, and it obeys instantly; the mind commands itself, and is resisted?' And he sees that the answer is that, in the latter case, 'it willeth not entirely; therefore doth it not command entirely . . . For were the will entire, it would not even command it to be, because it would already be.' To will, and not to do, then, is only partly to will, it is 'a disease of the mind' which saps its resolution and courage, leaving it full of wishes which, not fully willed, accomplish nothing. It is this will which is to be renounced. Not simply the sinful will, set on self-interest and self-indulgence, the captive of the passions and emotions, but the irresolute, feeble, halting will which, as it were, ever stands at the cross-roads, unable to take a step even on the road it wishes to follow.

To surrender oneself entirely to God, this is what renouncing one's own will means, without any reservations or compromises. For we cannot serve two masters, although we so often attempt this impossible thing, passing, as says Père Lallemant, 'entire years and often all our life hesitating as to whether we will give ourselves entirely to God, reserving to ourselves many affections, plans, hopes, desires, and pretensions, which we are unwilling to give up, but which prevent that perfect emptiness of spirit which disposes us to be entirely possessed by God . . . Encumbered by love of self, blinded by ignorance, held back by false fears, we dare not take the final step; and from fear of being miserable, are always miserable.'

This abiding in a wishing, rather than a willing, frame of mind is often due to our mind being more centred on what we may have to give up than upon what we shall receive. 'Give, and it will be given to you. A good measure, pressed down, shaken together, running over, will be put into your lap.'[34] How much more, then, shall God give to you? The truth is that it is just what we retain that we lose; what we give freely and generously comes back to us in a manner and degree it never before possessed. Such a giving of oneself to God, St Benedict will teach us, must be one, motivated not by emotion or impulse but by a clear sight of all that it implies. What he has to say as to the manner in which an aspirant to the religious life is to be received has its lessons for any one who would obey the 'Follow me' of Jesus.

'To him that newly comes to conversion, let not an easy entrance be granted.' The firmness of his intention, the quality of his patience and of his endurance of difficulties must be tested. Once admitted he is to be watched as to whether 'he truly seeks God, and is zealous for the work of God, for obedience, and humiliations. Let there be set before him all the hard and rugged ways by which we walk towards God'. The Holy Rule is read and explained to him 'that he may know to what he is entering'. Then only, after a lengthy time of probation, if he, 'having deliberated with himself, promises to keep all things, and to observe everything that is commanded him, may he be received into the community'.

The church would be in a very different position in the world today if those who came to conversion of manners,[35] and desired to enter into full membership of the Body of Christ, were treated in somewhat the same manner, as, indeed, is done in the mission field. What is easily gained is lightly treated, and if there is often so little difference between professing Christians and non Christians, it is because the former have not had set before them, and deliberated upon, the obligations and consequences of the Christian life. There has not been any real, chosen, willed, act of surrender, no renouncing of one's own will, no acceptance of a law to be obeyed and a warfare to be engaged in. Is this true of me? Am I one of those who 'sit at ease in Zion' instead of 'taking up the strong and bright weapons of obedience in order to fight for the Lord Christ, our true King'?

Friday of the Second Week in Lent

The strong weapons of obedience

'Take up the strong and bright weapons of obedience.' Doubtless St Benedict is speaking of the monk's obedience to his abbot, an obedience which is required of him since the abbot 'is believed to hold the place of Christ in the monastery'. But this is only one form of that obedience which is demanded of every Christian, and without which the Christian life cannot exist. All through holy Scripture we are taught the necessity and value of obedience, not only to God and his church but to all those to whom God has committed something of his magisterial authority. 'Obey them that have rule over you', 'Children, obey your parents', 'Servants, obey in all things', run the apostolic injunctions. Had not our Lord himself been obedient to Mary and Joseph, to the precepts of the ancient law, as well as to the will of his eternal Father? Had he not taught that obedience was to be rendered to the Scribes and Pharisees who sat in Moses' seat?[36] 'Therefore, do whatever they teach you and follow it; but do not do as they do, for they do not practice what they teach.'[37] Still more, was it not by his obedience that humanity had to be redeemed from the consequences of the first disobedience? 'For as by one man's disobedience many were made sinners, so by the obedience of one shall many be made righteous', by him who 'though he were a Son, yet learned he obedience by the things which he suffered; and being made perfect, became the author of eternal salvation unto all them that obey him'. St Augustine says that obedience is the greatest of virtues, the mother and source of all virtues, and, indeed, this is so. For it is the expression of faith, without which faith is dead, as says St James; of hope, since without obedience what dare we hope for from God; and of charity, for 'Those who love me will keep my words'. It is by obedience that faith leads to understanding, 'Any who will to do his will, shall know of the doctrine, whether it be of God, or whether I speak of myself'. It is by obedience that we proclaim whose we are, and whom we serve. 'Know ye not, that to whom ye yield yourselves servants to obey, his servants ye are to whom ye obey whether of sin unto death, or of obedience unto righteousness?' Let us not deceive ourselves into imagining that we can ever be free from that law of service which is inherent in our very nature. There can be no question as to whether we shall be servants or not, the only question is, whom shall we serve? But of all the masters whom we are free to choose, there is but one whose service leads not to the servitude of slaves, but to the freedom of sons and daughters in their Father's house. For he who proclaimed himself to be the truth has said, 'Very truly, I tell you, everyone who commits sin is a slave to sin. The slave does not have a permanent place in the household; the son has a place there forever. So if the Son makes you free, you will be free indeed.'[38]

Why does St Benedict speak of 'the strong and bright *weapons* of obedience'? Because it is by obedience to Christ alone that we can fight our way out of the servitude in which our disobedience has enslaved us. Sin may be forgiven in a moment, but the habit and the effects of sin can be overcome only by repeated facts of obedience to God's commands. And in the chapter on obedience our saint recounts the qualities by which this weapon 'is kept strong and bright', and wielded bravely in the service of our true King.

Obedience, he says, must be instant, without delay, 'fulfilled in the swiftness of the fear of God, by those upon whom presses the desire of attaining eternal life'. Almighty God has issued his commands, which are not for his good but for ours, and he must not be kept waiting. Moreover, who does not know that, as says the proverb, 'He who hesitates is lost'? The victory over temptation is most easily won in the moment it is perceived. Even if, as may be the case, the enemy is not at once put to flight, a decisive refusal at the outset is a tremendous source of strength. In the Prologue to the Rule, St Benedict speaks of him 'who has brought the malignant evil one to naught, casting him out of his heart with all his suggestions, having taken his bad thoughts, *while they were yet young*, and dashed them down upon Christ'. There must no parleying with the enemy, no listening to the insidious suggestions with which he would blind the soul, no yielding to the movement of interior passions, no admittance to the foe who clamours at the gate. For 'out of the heart proceed evil thoughts'[39] and it is there that the first motions of evil desires must be crushed, lest drawn away from God of our 'own lusts and enticed, then when lust hath conceived it bringeth forth sin; and sin, when it is finished, bringeth forth death'.

So 'with the ready step of obedience are we to follow by our deeds the voice of him who commands' thereby 'choosing the narrow way which leadeth unto life, living not by our own will, nor obeying our own desires and pleasures', and fulfilling the word of our Lord, 'I came not to do mine own will, but the will of him who sent me'. It is, continues the saint, such obedience which is 'acceptable to God, and dear unto men': obedience rendered 'not tardily or lukewarmly, nor with murmuring', but with such obedience which is 'acceptable to God, and dear unto men': obedience rendered 'not tardily, nor lukewarmly, nor with murmuring', but with 'goodwill, for God loveth a cheerful giver'.

To be a Catholic is pre-eminently to be under authority, recognising that we cannot, and must not, please ourselves as to what we shall believe or do. A faith revealed by God and taught by his church demands his whole assent, the 'obedience of faith'. We are not free to pick and choose, accepting only what commends itself to us, or to run after strange human doctrines which are incompatible with the faith of the church. A worship is prescribed for us, that of the Mass, ordained and commanded by our Lord himself. The commandments of God and of the church require our obedience, to withhold which is to sin. And only by such ready and constant obedience do we renounce our own will, refuse to be governed by sentiment and mere emotion, and manifest a true love for God. For it is said, 'If you love me, keep my commandments.'[40]

Let us turn to the 119th Psalm and see in the words of one who lived before the Incarnation what the law, the commandments, the testimonies, and the statutes of God ought to be to him. Then let us, with the Psalmist, acknowledge, 'Thou hast charged that we shall diligently keep Thy commandments', and pray that we may have that 'fervent desire', that 'love and delight', that studious attention to, and understanding of, the divine law, that so we may 'keep it with [our] whole heart', learn 'to hate all evil ways, and delight in that which is good', and so to come to that blessedness of those who 'walk in the law of the Lord', and to that 'glorious liberty of the children of God' which is the reward of those who 'run in the way of his commandments'.

There is a war on

'Take up the strong and bright weapons of obedience, in order to fight for Christ, our true King.'

To submit oneself to the 'obedience of faith' is not to seek an escape from the stern realities of life in this world, rather it is to turn and face them with an understanding and courage which can never be theirs who, rapt in 'the sloth of disobedience', are the true 'escapists' of every age. There is nothing in the teaching of Jesus Christ and his apostles and saints to justify the idea that in becoming a Christian in the fullest sense of the word one has the right to expect immunity from trouble, difficulty, conflict and struggle. On the contrary, we are warned that all this will be intensified, that if we come to serve the Lord we must prepare ourselves for temptation, that in the world we shall have tribulation, that we come to enrol ourselves under the standard of one who has said, 'I came not to send peace but a sword,' and who demands from us such a discipleship, such a denial of self, such sacrifice, as will test every faculty of our being. For it is to no temple of peace, no life of comfortable security and repose, no lotus-eater's paradise, that Christ calls us, but to a stern, unremitting warfare, in which blows and wounds, constant vigilance, exact obedience, and untiring combat with enemies, both without and within are to be expected. And with this he promises us sufficient grace to arm us against all our foes; the certainty of his abiding presence within us; our daily rations of heavenly food, and of all that is necessary for our temporal life; and the assurance of victory. 'In the world you face persecution. But take courage; I have conquered the world!' 'To everyone who conquers, I will give permission to eat from the tree of life that is in the paradise of God . . . Be faithful until death, and I will give you the crown of life'.[41]

We do not, then, embrace the Christian life in order to enjoy the privileges of religion, but to use them in the prosecution of a holy war; not to 'sit at ease in Zion', but to go forth armed *cap-a-pie* to the conflict with the world, the flesh, and the devil. No neutrality is possible; we must either fight or become quislings, traitors who go over to the enemy, and become his subservient slaves. 'His servants are ye whom ye obey.' 'Ye cannot serve two masters.' But you must serve one.

'Our hearts, therefore, and our bodies, must be made ready to fight under the holy obedience of his commands,' says St Benedict, who was neither a Platonist nor a Manichean. The former held that the soul alone was important, the body being merely a temporary 'prison' from which the soul must free itself. The latter believed that the body was an evil thing in itself, a belief which, to some degree, persisted in Puritanism. But the Catholic faith teaches us that soul and body are essential to human nature, that neither the soul alone, nor the body alone, is the person, and that the whole person, body as well as soul, is to be employed in the worship and service of God. The common expression 'saving one's soul' must not be understood to exclude the body, for nothing that we do, or is done to us is done or suffered by soul or body alone. We can no more worship without our bodies than we can work without our souls. And we are saved by our acts, aided by the grace of God, and the body is the soul in act, as says St Thomas Aquinas. The common teaching of the church that the souls in purgatory cannot do anything for themselves is, to some extent, based on this fact, as is also the teaching that our final and complete perfection is attained only in the reunion of soul and body of which we confess our faith and expectation. *Exspecto*, I look for, expect, 'the resurrection of the dead, and the life of the world to come'.

It is not surprising, then, to find that the New Testament has indeed more to say about the body than the soul, though, of course, no mention of the body (as, for example, in St Paul's 'I appeal to you therefore, brothers and sisters, by the mercies of God, to present your bodies as a living sacrifice, holy and acceptable to God, which is your spiritual worship') implies that the soul has no part in such an offering. The soul, with its faculties of mind and will, may be considered as the priest, already dedicated to the service of God, who makes this living, rational sacrifice.

'Our hearts and our bodies must be made ready.' And who does not know that the latter is as difficult as the former if not more so? Even when the spirit is willing, the flesh is weak and, in our case, not merely naturally weak but positively rebellious. 'For what the flesh desires is opposed to the Spirit, and what the Spirit desires is opposed to the flesh; for these are opposed to each other.'[42] By 'the flesh' we are to understand, not the physical body, but all that lower part of the self in which lie the passions, good in themselves but needing to be subjected to, to be ordered, controlled, and directed by, the spirit. The words of a mountain climber may well be quoted in this connection. It is when the body plays its part in the attainment of an ideal that the flesh and spirit cease to be contrary one to the other. The only perfect moments of life are those in which the two are one.

Our warfare begins within ourselves. Like the soldier we have to submit ourselves to discipline, training; we must be equipped with the 'weapons of our warfare' and learn how to use them. The rebellion within must be dealt with before we attack the enemy without, or we shall find ourselves betrayed from within, as have many nations in wartime. 'Fight self,' said St Catherine of Genoa, 'and you need fear no other foe,' and a young soldier has told us how he, and others, found it necessary 'to win victories over ourselves, before we won them over our enemies'.

And whether the field of our warfare be within or without,

let us not be astonished or discouraged, to find it not only one of difficulty but one in which we shall suffer weariness, wounds, and defeat at times. For we fight for our true King who was weary and wounded, and is oft-times weary and wounded in his servants, the members of his body. But his wounds shine gloriously in heaven, and if we treat ours with penitence and renewed confidence and perseverance, they shall minister to our final triumph, the triumph of those who did not refuse to fight, nor ran away, but died at their post, scarred but facing the foe.

Third Sunday in Lent

Christ, our true King

'To fight for Christ, our true King.'

It is always difficult for the human mind to keep an even balance both in belief and practice. To be impressed with one aspect of a certain truth may lead us to forget or minimise another aspect equally important. It is thus that the great heresies concerning the person of our Lord arose; and in our own time, in which Christian truths have been subjected to the sentimentality which has invaded religion, an overemphasis on the truth expressed in the words 'Gentle Jesus, meek and mild' has done much to obscure the fact of his royal kingship, his divine majesty, his absolute sovereignty. No one would question the gentleness, the meekness, and mildness of Jesus, but these terms as applied to him mean much more than they do in common usage. For his gentleness is not that of an indulgent weakness but of an immense strength; his meekness, if that of the Lamb of God, is no less that of the Lion of the tribe of Judah; his mildness but one expression of a fire of love which, if it warm and comfort, no less consumes.

All through the New Testament these two complementary truths are kept in view, as they are in the prophetic utterances which foretell the coming of the Messiah, at once 'a lamb led to the slaughter' and a king who shall reign in righteousness. If the angelic message to Joseph announces the birth of the Saviour, that to Mary proclaims that 'he shall reign over the house of Jacob for ever; and of his kingdom there shall be no end'. The Magi come from afar to find and acknowledge one who is 'the King of the Jews'. During the public mission the multitudes are struck with the authority with which Jesus speaks and the power with which he acts. They are ready to accept him as their king, though, as is still the case with many, their ideas of what this implies are far other than his. Against his tender gentleness with sinners and with his apostles' lack of faith and understanding, must be set his stern denunciation of Scribes and Pharisees, and the manner in which he drives out from the temple courts those who dishonour his Father's house. To Pilate's question, 'Are you the King of the Jews?'[43] he replies in the affirmative, whilst repudiating the title in the sense his accusers had used it, 'My kingdom is not of this world'; and to the governor's somewhat scornful reply, 'So you are a king?' he states the foundation of truth upon which his kingdom rests, and which justifies his claim to our obedience. 'You say that I am a king. For this I was born, and for this I came into the world, to testify to the truth. Everyone who belongs to the truth listens to my voice.'[44] And when we come to the last words of the New Testament in the Apocalypse of St John, every page rings with the sovereignty of him to whom has been committed 'all power in heaven and on earth', who is 'King of kings and Lord of lords',[45] before whom every knee must bow.

The Preface of the Mass for the Feast of Christ the King sums up the truth which the feast celebrates, giving thanks to God 'who didst anoint thine only begotten Son, our Lord Jesus Christ, with the oil of gladness, to be a priest for ever, and King over all the world; that, offering himself a sacrifice of peace upon the altar of the cross, he might accomplish the sacrament of the redemption of mankind; and when all creation should have been submitted to his rule, might deliver up to thine infinite majesty an eternal and universal kingdom, a kingdom of truth and life, a kingdom of holiness and grace, a kingdom of justice, love and peace'.

This truth of the kingship of Jesus Christ lies at the heart of the faith and practice of a Christian. To all too many people the Christian faith often appears as a helpful and comforting thing, the particular truths and practices of which they are free to choose, such as commend themselves to the individual.

That it is an imperative, a demand for belief in and obedience to a divine authority, an allegiance to a supreme Sovereign, whose word it conveys, whose law it promulgates, as an absolute necessity for human salvation, hardly occurs to them. So deep and widespread is this attitude that today children of professing Christian parents ask, 'Why should we believe Jesus Christ any more than any other person? How do we know that what he says is true?' To attempt to teach the faith to the upper forms of schools today is to face an atmosphere of ignorance and apathy which reflects only too plainly that of the homes from which children come. The danger of religious toleration is that no religion, save in the vaguest sense of the word, is tolerable.

To be a Christian is to recognise that one is a subject responsible for rendering worship, allegiance, loyalty, service to Jesus Christ, 'His Divine Majesty', as St Teresa loved to think of him. It is to see religion as one, and the highest, expression of justice – the means by which we render to God what is due to him. This may not always be either pleasurable or convenient, any more than is paying one's bills. The point is that it is necessary, an obligation, to fail in fulfilling which is an injustice, a disobedience, a sin. It is to see the faith as a divine revelation made by God and conveyed to the world through his church to which authority and power has been given, 'to teach all nations . . . whatsoever I have commanded you'[46] and of which he who is the truth has said, 'He that heareth you heareth me, and he that despiseth you despiseth me'. It is to walk, not in one's own way, but 'in the law of the Lord', who has declared himself to be the way, the truth and the life, 'one who is not merely the greatest of human teachers and lawgivers', but the eternal 'Word made flesh', whom God 'hath made to sit at his right hand in heavenly places, far above all rule, and authority, and power, and dominion, and every name that is named, not only in this world, but in that which is to come; and hath put all things in subjection under his feet, and gave him to be head over all things to the church which is his body, the fullness, the completeness of him that filleth all things'.

There is no greater act of faith, nor one more necessary today, than to believe in, and witness to, both by worship and service, the kingship of Jesus Christ. For never was it more denied, questioned, and scorned; never was it more possible that we in this country may have to witness to it, not in the quiet and comfort of our churches, or upon our knees, but in the face of the materialism and selfishness which is the daily enemy against which the modern Christian is called upon to fight. A few years ago the writer was rebuked for preaching such a possibility to a London congregation. Today the reality of it is so near to us that we may well take heed to St Benedict's words, 'Our hearts and our bodies must be made ready to fight under his commands', yes, and if need be, to suffer in the fighting.

Our enemies, and how to meet them

'To fight for Christ, our true King.'

This is the daily battle of faith against temptation which is part of the life of every Christian. But we need to remember that we engage in it not, so to speak, on God's behalf, but in his power. The infinite resources of grace are there for us to call upon however hard the conflict, in the assurance of a victory already won in the decisive battle of Calvary.

But what and who is it we are to fight, and how must the combat be waged? To lack such knowledge is to be unprepared and unable to fight successfully; to find ourselves in a position which is much harder to retrieve than it would have been to hold. To this end, the mind must be enlightened and informed by both reason and faith, for a spiritual vision alone will make us conscious of the fact that 'our wrestling is not against flesh and blood, but against principalities, against powers, against the world rulers of darkness, against spiritual hosts of wickedness in heavenly places': enemies of immense, but not invincible, power.

The weapons employed may be in the hands of people, commerce, our own culture and traditions: the good things of this world may become as poisoned wells to us, the very faculties of our nature may play the role of fifth columnists; but it is no new war in which, as members of the Church Militant we take our part. It is that age-old conflict engaged in by people of faith since the beginning of time and into which Christ calls all those whom 'he is not ashamed to call his brethren', those who 'keep the commandments of God, and hold testimony of Jesus' in their hearts.

We do not fight against a simple, identifiable enemy but

one manifest in more subtle and deceptive ways: beguiling us through the apparently good and even holy things in our lives, luring us on through the good intentions with which the road to hell is paved, turning the good of our nature into rebellion and our noble aspirations into self-serving delusions.

St Benedict has spoken already of the need of that immediate refusal to parley with our evil thoughts, and here we may now return to the central truth that temptation is better overcome by our turning at once to God than by directing ourselves against the temptation. The *Veni Creator* is a more powerful weapon than *Retro me, Satanas*, it has been said, and the author of *The Cloud of Unknowing* bids those in temptation to 'try and look, as it were, over their shoulders, seeking another thing, the which thing is God'. For the victory over temptation is to those who put on the whole armour of God, 'so that you may be able to withstand on that evil day, and having done everything, to stand firm'.[47]

'To stand', for this is the victory, which so often does not consist in the immediate routing of the enemy. 'Resist the devil, and he will flee from you.' Yes; but the resistance must often be long and obstinate. So St Paul will teach us that victory consists more in endurance than in putting the enemy to flight. 'God is faithful, in that he will not suffer you to be tempted above that ye are able; but will with the temptation make a way of escape. *That ye may be able to bear it*.' And St James bids us, 'Count it all joy when ye fall into divers temptations; knowing this, that the trying of your faith worketh patience. But let patience have her perfect work, that ye may be perfect and entire, wanting nothing . . . Blessed is the man that endureth temptation, for when he is tried, he shall receive the crown of life, which the Lord hath promised to them that love him.'

What is most needed in this conflict is confidence in God, the remembrance of such words as 'No weapon that is formed against thee shall prosper', 'The Lord is on my right hand, therefore I shall not fall'. 'I can do all things through

Christ who strengtheneth me', and who has said, 'My grace is sufficient for thee.' We do not fight alone, nor is the battle merely ours; it is God's, and he has promised 'I will never leave thee, nor forsake thee.' It is Christ's, who says, 'Ye are they who have continued with me in my temptations,' for those which we suffer are aimed at him who dwells within the souls of his children, and demands of their enemy, 'why persecutest thou me?'

So must we take up his weapons, and fight in the power of his Spirit. 'For though we walk in the flesh, we do not war according to the flesh: (for the weapons of our warfare are not carnal, but mighty through God to the pulling down of strongholds), casting down imaginations, and every high thing which exalteth itself against the knowledge of God.' Nothing less than the 'whole armour of God' will enable us to overcome, nor in this life can it be laid aside, for the holy war against self, the world, and the devil must be fought out 'to the last gasp of truth and loyalty'.

Who shall rest upon his holy hill?

'Behold, in his loving kindness the Lord shows unto us the way of life . . . But let us ask the Lord with the prophet, "Lord, who shall dwell within thy tabernacle, and who shall rest upon thy holy hill?"'

St Benedict has spoken already of the first steps by which we are to enlist in the army of the living God, of the return to him by the labour of obedience, the renunciation of our own wills, the obligation of serving God 'with the good things he has given us', the need of earnest prayer that he will perfect that good work which, by his grace, he has begun in us. Now, before he goes further, he reminds us of what should be the character of one who would serve God. 'The Lord, seeking his own [worker] in the multitude of the people, says again, "Who is the [one] that will have life, and desires to see good days?" And if you, hearing him, answer, "I am he," God says to you, "If thou wilt have true and everlasting life, keep thy tongue from evil, and thy lips that they speak no guile. Turn from evil, and do good; seek peace, and pursue it. And when you have done these things, my eyes will be upon you, and my ears will be open to your prayers; and before you call upon me, I will say unto you, behold, I am here."' Then he bids us ask the question at the head of this chapter, and to 'hear the Lord answering' and showing to us the way to his tabernacle, and saying: 'he that walks without stain and works justice; he that speaks truth in his heart, that hath not done guile with his tongue; he that has done no evil to his neighbour, and has not taken up a reproach against his neighbour.' We shall find echoes of this in the chapter on 'The Instruments of Good Works', to be considered later.

Let us mark well that the Prologue, together with the first seven chapters of the Holy Rule, are all concerned with the inner life and character of the servant of God. Not until this has been stated and defined does the saint speak of the outward practices of the Christian life, which he gathers up in worship, study and work. He would have us realise that it is not what we do but the end for which, and the spirit in which, we do it that is of first importance, that it is what we are which God regards. 'The Lord does not see as mortals see; they look on the outward appearance, but the Lord looks on the heart.'[48] For in the words of our Lord, 'Out of the abundance of the heart the mouth speaks. The good person brings good things out of a good treasure, and the evil person brings evil things out of an evil treasure.'[49] No exterior compliance with the obligations of religion can compensate for, or be accepted in lieu of, the offering of 'a pure and contrite heart'.[50] That is a truth which is constantly repeated both in the Old and the New Testament. The guard of the heart, the care of the interior, is our primary task; only as we fulfil this shall we come near to bearing that character of which the Lord has spoken.

To read that summary of what God looks for in us is to become conscious of how little we have attained to it, a consciousness which may be followed by the temptation to doubt whether it is even possible. But we must remember that it represents an ideal of perfection, the value of which lies in the fact that it is almost out of our reach in this life, but that it is only in reaching after it, not in lowering it, that we can approximate to it.

Perfection in this life consists in tending toward perfection, more in aiming at the ideal than in attaining it. No one has come nearer to it than the saints, and what they thought of their efforts is well expressed by St Paul: 'Not that I have already obtained this or have already reached the goal . . . I do not consider that I have made it my own; but this one thing I do: forgetting what lies behind and straining forward to what lies ahead, I press on toward the goal for the prize of the heavenly call of God in Christ Jesus. Let those of us then who are mature be of the same mind.'[51]

It is not important, nor is it possible, for us to see much of our progress, or measure it. But we can see to it that we are not standing still or going back, that we are using the means by which we may progress and avoiding the things which would hinder us. Are we actually and definitely turning from 'every appearance of evil', and occupying ourselves with doing good? Are we endeavouring to keep ourselves 'unspotted from the world', and to act justly toward all people? Do we strive not only to keep our tongues from evil and our lips that they speak no guile, but also to 'speak truth in our hearts', 'be truthful with ourselves'? Are we positively (not merely negatively) seeking, pursuing peace; and so doing no evil to our neighbours, speaking no ill of them, or (even commoner fault) 'taking up' and passing on no reproach against them? It is such questions which are much more necessary in our self-examination than those which are concerned with 'wandering thoughts' in prayer, or the omission of pious practices which are not of obligation.

And if we find little to accuse ourselves of in these matters St Benedict will warn us 'not to be puffed up with our own good works, but, knowing that the good which is in them comes, not from ourselves, but from the Lord, magnify the Lord who works in us, saying with the psalmist, "Not to us, O Lord, not to us, but to your name give glory",[52] or with St Paul, "By the grace of God I am what I am",[53] so far as any good is concerned'.

Girded with faith

'Having our loins, therefore, girded with faith and the performance of good works let us walk in his paths.'

The Christian is a pilgrim who has here 'no abiding city, but seeks one to come,'[54] and here St Benedict states what is his first and continuing need. For 'he that cometh to God must believe that he is, and that he is a rewarder of them that diligently seek him'. And to faith must be added good works, without which, says St James, 'faith is dead', and of no more value than that of the devils who 'also believe, and tremble'.[55]

The Christian walk is a journey, not a promenade; a pilgrimage actuated by faith in the existence of a definite goal, and the desire to attain it. That faith is not founded in sentiment or feeling, but in a rational conviction, a sight of the mind which, raised above its merely natural capacity by the gift of faith, moves us to undertake this journey 'as seeing him who is invisible'. In its elementary form, faith is an assent to the authority of God speaking through his church, an assent based on the evidence of a witness upon whom reason assures us we can safely rely. Proofs of various kinds, arguments, our own and others' experience, may confirm and justify our faith, but they do not create it, nor does the intrinsic truth of Christian mysteries. The sole foundation upon which faith rests is the revealed word of God to which we render belief, and 'the obedience of faith'[56] to the supreme truth himself, who can neither deceive nor be deceived.

Faith in God, and in all that he has revealed, is necessary because our minds are incapable of comprehending and fully understanding the mysteries of the kingdom of God.

There is nothing extraordinary in this, for our minds are equally incapable of grasping the mysteries of the world about us, and especially the greatest of them – ourselves. We live and walk by faith in mundane matters no less than in spiritual ones. We accept what we are taught by the experts in the various sciences, and, indeed, too often what we are told by those who have little claim to be experts, especially in the sphere of religion. But to be a Christian is to become the disciple of a divine master, one who has founded and given power and authority to his church to 'teach all nations',[57] and has said, 'He that heareth you heareth me, and he that despiseth you despiseth me.' It is impossible to believe that these and similar words of our Lord should have been intended for the apostles alone. The one link between A. D. 33 and our time is that church which has ever claimed to be the body of Christ through which his truth and grace are conveyed to every age.

Faith, then, is an act of the intellect accepting truths of the divine order which can be known only by a divine revelation. Such an acceptance leads to a growing understanding of such truths, both by the church as a whole and by the individual. The faith itself 'once for all delivered to the saints' does not grow or develop, but each age of the church reveals a growing apprehension of its content and meaning, a process of fuller understanding which may be seen in the writings of the New Testament, and has gone on ever since the apostolic age. So is it, also, with anyone who, taking God at his word, and rendering to him 'the obedience of faith', comes to a certain knowledge of divine realities, as did St John, whose first letter rings with the certainty of one who knows, repeating again and again, not 'we believe' but 'we know'.

For, in the words of Aquinas, 'faith is a kind of participation in God's truth', enabling us to share in God's own knowledge. It 'gives persistence and stability to our apprehension' by 'withdrawing the mind from the domain of nature and sense and setting it on the foundation of things intelligible'. By faith our feet are set upon that rock of which the psalmist prays, 'O set me up upon the rock which is higher than I',[58] and of which our Lord speaks, 'Everyone then who hears these words of mine and acts on them will be like a wise man who built his house on rock.'[59]

Further, says Aquinas, 'faith draws divine things to us' and causes them 'to abide in us', giving us possession of the very things in which we believe. It is not with our eyes, but with our minds illumined by faith, that true hearts discern the presence of Jesus veiled from all other sight beneath the forms of bread and wine. It is not with the mouth that the guilty slave eats the body of the Lord, but with that saving faith which receives the living bread in the innermost depths of the soul. It is by faith that, deprived of sensible consolation and experience, we go on worshipping, praying, enduring 'as seeing him who is invisible'. For faith is not feeling, not touch, or taste, or sight of the senses, but that which survives and triumphs when these are absent; that which, however much it may be aided by exterior and sensible things, learns not to depend on them but to walk securely and confidently, even when 'the foundations of the world are out of course' and the soul experiences a 'blackout' in which no ray of light, save that of faith, shows where its feet should tread.

This is the faith, ever exercised in loving obedience, which 'overcomes the world', for it lives not on bread alone but on the living Word, 'the food of the strong', the comfort of the weak, the defence of the tempted, the companion of the lonely, the might of those who are persecuted for righteousness' sake, the blessedness of the persevering, for it is this faith which unites the soul to God its Beatitude.

The performance of good works

'The performance of good works . . . If we wish to dwell in the tabernacle of his kingdom, we shall by no means reach it unless we run thither by our good deeds.'

It will be clear already that St Benedict is neither a fideist nor a pietist; there is nothing of the modern, sentimentalist conception, either of the religious or of the Christian life, in the Holy Rule. He is severely practical, discreet, sober, knowing that he legislates not for those in whom the religious instinct is strongly developed but for ordinary men and women who, convinced of the facts and claims of the Christian religion, set out to embody it in their lives. So here he insists that 'faith without works is dead';[60] belief must be translated into practice, since it is by human acts performed according to reason and faith, and aided by grace, that we deserve to reach the end for which we were created.

The enumeration, in a later chapter, of the instruments of good works reveals that by 'good deeds' the saint does not mean simply specifically religious acts, such as worship and prayer, but every act which can rightly be termed human, and as such has to do with humanity's final end. We do not run towards God merely, or even chiefly, by multiplying our religious exercises and devotions, but by a Christianising of all our actions, be they of the mind or body. For thoughts, the immanent acts of the mind, are the source from which our exterior actions flow, and by their potent influence transform the very fabric of our lives and characters. 'As a man thinks, so is he.'

The road to hell is paved with good intentions which are not translated into action – do not become good works. And what is a good work? It is a willed act, performed according to the dictates of reason and faith, and so truly human. Many of our common actions are of the animal order, but to be acts of a human being they must be rational, willed, free, and directed toward an end suitable to our nature. An act based merely on impulse, sentiment, feelings, or any other passion is not a truly human act. Nor is one which is forced upon us by some exterior power which we are unable to resist. The essence of a human act lies in its being deliberate, controlled, one of which we are in control and therefore one for which we are personally responsible.

For an act to be good it must have some known good as its end, and so must contribute to the good of the one who performs it. For only the good adds to our nature and perfects it. Hence the need of the knowledge of the good, for the will ever tends toward, and seeks, that which the mind conceives as good. Everyone knows how easy it is to be deceived by appearances, and by the influence of the passions, each intent on its own satisfaction without regard for the good of the whole person. A sound mind, a right judgement, a single eye, the power of discrimination between apparent and real goods, all these lie behind and determine our good actions. On these follow the deliberate choice of the good perceived (often involving a deliberate and sometimes painful rejection of an attractive apparent good) and, even more important, the choice and the use of the means by which the good is to be accomplished or attained.

None of this is possible save to those who see its importance and necessity, and are willing to submit themselves to the discipline and training which it involves. A clear mental sight, the power of forming right judgements, the command of the will, these are not things with which we are born, or which we can come by easily and without effort. They do not descend upon us from heaven merely because we wish and ask for them, but only as we are prepared to work for them, fight for them, just as we have to do for everything worth having in this life.

The complacent ignorance of many pious persons who apparently have never realised that the mind is the greatest natural gift God has conferred upon them, and the common superstition that religion consists in churchgoing, outside of which the leisured spend their days in fatuous and useless pursuits, and their more fortunate neighbours in hard work, none of which is thought of as having any connection with religion, is largely responsible for the irreligious outlook of the young of our time. The questions which children ask, the opinions they express, reveal the appalling state of the homes, often professedly Christian, from which they come.

By good deeds we run toward God, and by nothing else. And run we must – there can be no loitering or standing about in the Christian life. Not to go forward is to go back, to lose ground, to waste time, to endanger our souls. We are safe only when we are moving, for movement is the sign of life, the expression of desire, of the sense of an end to be attained. 'Incessant growth is a condition of perfect living personality.' And our running towards God is not simply a running to God, it is a becoming like God, in which by the doing of good deeds we share in the Supreme Good, and in our human manner become perfect, even as our Father who is in heaven is perfect.

Friday of the Third Week in Lent

The instruments of good works

The fourth chapter of the Holy Rule, entitled 'What are the Instruments of Good Works?' illustrates both the statement of Bossuet that the Rule is 'an epitome of Christianity' and the mind of St Benedict in regarding the monastic life as one way of fulfilling the precepts which are binding upon each of the faithful. For, with one exception (that which speaks of obedience to the abbot), every one of these instruments is as necessary to the Christian living in the world as to the monk in the cloister. If these 'tools of the spiritual craft', as the saint names them, 'are to be used by the monk in the workshop of the cloister of the monastery', no less are they to be in the hands of every one of us whose workshop is determined by our particular vocation, whatever this may be, since they concern our duty to God, our neighbour and our self.

'First Instrument: in the first place to love the Lord God with all one's heart, all one's soul and all one's strength.' In the first place, for to love God above all things is a debt of nature no less than of grace; and to love God means to choose him, to prefer him before all things, to give him the first and unique place in our lives. The fact that we are commanded to love God shows plainly that it is not a love of feelings which is meant primarily, but one of the will, a deliberate choice of God which may (and often does) exist without any such movement of affection as normally accompanies love for human beings. For this is something we cannot always command, as even the saints knew, whilst we can command our wills and manifest the truest love by faith, hope, and obedience. 'If you love me, keep my commandments.'[61] There is a test which we can each apply to ourselves, whatever our feelings may be.

To put God first in our thoughts and lives does not exclude, but rather includes, every right and legitimate love; indeed demands that we should love all that God loves, and as he loves. All that is excluded is any love for creatures which puts them in that first place which belongs to God alone, and that perversion of love which selfishly seeks to gain for oneself rather than to give to the object of love. For we must love as God loves, and God loves himself above all, since there is nothing above or beyond himself, nor anything so deserving of his love; and God loves his whole creation, since it is an effect of his love, and so loves it by ever bestowing good upon it, not as by seeking or gaining anything from it.

We do not need to make meticulous distinctions between love for God and love of creatures. To love what God loves, and as he loves it, is to love him from whom all its lovableness is derived. Did not our Lord love his friends, his country, the holy city and the flowers of the field? And this, enwrapped in his love for his eternal Father, whose well-loved creatures these were. If God is our first and abiding choice, we need not question whether, in loving our kinsfolk and friends, our country or the beauty of earth, we are or are not loving God above all. St Augustine, referring to the innumerable toys made by diverse arts and manufactures, in our clothing, shoes, utensils, and all sorts of works, which far exceed all necessary and moderate use and all pious meaning, speaks of those people who by inwardly following what they themselves make, inwardly forsake him by whom they were made. 'But I, my God and glory, do from hence also sing a hymn to thee, and do consecrate praise to him who consecrates me, because through those beautiful patterns which through [people's] souls are conveyed into their cunning hands, come from that beauty, which is above our souls, which my soul day and night longeth after.'

Wherever the mind discerns truth or goodness or beauty, there it sees something of God, and in praising and loving it, praises and loves the divine source from which it flows. We are often astonished at, and sometimes taunted with, the fact of the deep love, the goodness, and kindness shown by those who make little or no profession of religion, especially amongst the poor, whose charity often exceeds that of their more 'fortunate' and Christian neighbours. But this is to forget the truth, so insisted upon by the medieval theologians, that all people are by their very nature bound to love God above all, and in fact do so, even when unconscious of it. For what creature is there which does not seek its own good, creatures below humanity by a law of their nature, and humanity by intelligence and will? And in thus seeking that good which, rightly or wrongly, is conceived as the good which perfects them, bestows that happiness for which they insatiably crave, each seeks, however blindly, after God, the Supreme Good.

Sin itself is but the perversion of love, an act possible only to one in whom love has been implanted, and whose misery it is not to see its true good, and so to stumble blindly after it, stooping to the dust to find what lies above its head. Yet sin, though it diminish the good which God made human, cannot destroy it; even in hell it is still a good thing which has gone wrong, and now perceives and hates what it has lost beyond recall. But in this life the good cannot be entirely lost, and shines out in the lives and acts of many in whom, save for experience of it, one would hardly dream of looking for it. The writer can recall many an act of charity and kindness done to a stranger by rough 'hard-boiled' people in far-off lands, by poverty-stricken peasants on lonely mountain sides, by almost naked 'primitives' untouched by the dubious 'blessings' of civilisation, to whom he owes, as does every one who has travelled far and wide, debts which cannot be paid, and for which material payment has again and again been indignantly refused. It is from such experiences that one begins to understand our Lord's words, 'The publicans and harlots go into the kingdom of heaven before you',[62] and 'Just as you did it to one of the least of these who are members of my family, you did it to me'.[63]

'In the first place, to love God' for no other place is sufficient for him, or acceptable to him. And then, says Augustine, 'do what you will' for truly to love God is to have no will but his; to love him with the whole of one's self, mind, and will, bringing the rest of the faculties and passions a living sacrifice to love's altar. To love God – and why? Because he is God, what more should we ask? And how? Wholly, without limits, reservations, or half measures, but generously.

Saturday of the Third Week in Lent

The love of our neighbour

'THEN, thy neighbour as thyself.'

Not more than God, nor less than oneself. The measure and meaning of the second great commandment is to be found in the love of self. Yet are we not taught to hate self, to fight and overcome self, that self is our most dangerous enemy? Yes, and rightly so; but why? Because there is a self which is to be so loved that everything must be done to save it from that other self which would destroy it.

There is a self, a person, fashioned in the image and likeness of its creator, pronounced by him to be very good, and so loved by him as to be fitted and destined for union with himself. A self which is to be loved as God loves it, both for what he has made it by nature, and for what it may become by grace. A self which, despite the fact that it has fallen among thieves who have wounded and robbed it, has not lost its inherent goodness and dignity, nor forfeited the divine regard which, far from leaving it by the wayside to die, hastens to its rescue.

And there is an alien self which is to be hated, driven out from that abode in which God would dwell. A self which, like some corrupting disease which seizes upon the body, weakens and may destroy it if it be not cured, is capable of enfeebling and destroying the true self which must be loved if it is to be saved and rendered whole into the hands of its maker. The sick must love themselves if they are to regain their health; and, loving themselves, take every means, however painful, to that end.

To love oneself aright demands a right knowledge of what we are by creation and are destined to be by grace; not, as is too often imagined, to know merely what we have made ourselves by our sins. It is, in the words of Hugh of St Victor, to know our condition and place, what we owe to things above us and beneath us; and 'to ourselves, to understand what we have been made, how we should conduct ourselves, what we should do and not do'. For a true understanding of what sin is, and does, is possible only when we know him against whom we have sinned, the divinely created nature which has been weakened and perverted by sin, the future which sin has imperilled. How shall we set about the reformation of the image of God within our souls, save as we see the true image to whom we are to be conformed? Health is not regained by dwelling on disease, nor beauty by contemplating ugliness. 'Look unto me and be saved,' says our God.

To love oneself aright is to will all good to oneself, and so to take all steps necessary to procure it; and such is love of our neighbour. For, in words which have been attributed to St Bernard, 'He who seeks God's image in himself, seeks there his neighbour no less than himself; and finding it, finds it as it is in all mankind. If, then, thou seest thyself, thou seest me also, who art no other than thyself; and if thou lovest the image of God, then thou lovest me, as an image of God; and I also, loving God, love thee.'

To love our neighbours, then, is not necessarily to 'like' all that we see in them, any more than, unless we are very foolish, we like everything in ourselves. It is to see our neighbours as children of God, bearing his image, loved by him, created to be his for all eternity. It is to will them every good, and to do them whatever good lies within our power, especially to those whom God puts in our way as if he would say, 'Look after these for me'. It is to realise and act upon the teaching of our Lord in the parable of the sheep and the goats; to see in any one who needs our aid the living Christ who said, 'Just as you did it to one of the least of these who are members of my family, you did it to me.'[64] What St Benedict says about the reception of guests is applicable to all who come to us, 'Let all guests that come be received like Christ himself,' and, 'Let special care and solicitude be shown in the reception of the poor, because in them Christ is more received.' 'Received' – it is the word we use in speaking of our Communions wherein we show all reverence and honour to Jesus as he comes to us under the homely forms of bread and wine. But how many other disguises he has, equally deserving of our faith – and of our charity!

Having stated the two great commandments, St Benedict goes on to illustrate the second from those of the Old Law: 'Not to kill, not to commit adultery, not to steal, not to covet, not to bear false witness.' And before we absolve ourselves with regard to these, let us remember how our Lord gave them new content and meaning. Then 'to honour all [people], not to do unto another what one would not have done to oneself, not to render evil for evil, to do no wrong to any one, to love one's enemies, and to pray for them in the love of Christ, to hate [no one], not to render cursing for cursing but rather blessing, to relieve the poor, to clothe the naked, to visit the sick, to bury the dead, to help in affliction, to console the sorrowful'.

But how very elementary! we exclaim. Surely more than this is expected of religious. Yes, much more, but not of religious only, but of every Christian. And before we think about scaling the heights, we do well to examine how we walk on the flats. It is not ecstasies which make saints, but common, lowly duties done well and perseveringly; and St John of the Cross will remind us that 'at eventide they will examine thee in love'. It should be the first subject of our daily *examen* of conscience.

FOURTH SUNDAY IN LENT

What things we must avoid

Some of the Instruments of Good Works are dealt with in other chapters of this book; here we shall confine ourselves to those which remain.

'To keep aloof from worldly actions': actions, that is, dictated by worldly motives, worldly standards and ends. 'Do not love the world or the things in the world. The love of the Father is not in those who love the world.'[65] The second sentence explains the first. St John is not speaking of the world of nature, which God loves, pronounced very good, and gave to us for our good. No, 'God must be glad when one loves his world so much'. What we are to reject is the world which ' lieth in darkness', the world of 'the lust of the flesh, and the lust of the eyes, and the vainglory of life', the world which is contrary to the 'will of God which abideth for ever'.

'To prefer nothing to the love of Christ.' The love of Christ for us, our love for him, what shall we, what do we, prefer to this? 'Who will separate us from the love of Christ?' asks the Apostle. 'Will hardship, or distress, or persecution, or famine, or nakedness, or peril, or sword? . . . No, in all these things we are more than conquerors through him who loved us.'[66] Nothing can separate us, save our own wills preferring aught before him.

'Not to gratify anger.' He does not say, 'Not to be angry,' for there are occasions when anger is justified. But not to gratify anger, to give way to it, to take pleasure in it, so, 'not to harbour a desire for revenge, not to foster guile in one's heart, not to make a feigned peace, not to forsake charity', but 'to utter truth from heart and mouth, not to render evil for evil, to do no wrong to any one, to love one's enemies, not to be proud', for therein lies the root of sin against God and our neighbour, the source of all uncharity.

'You are exasperatingly charitable to wicked people,' she said. 'Well, my dear, I try to behave to them as I trust God will behave to me.'

We pass to a list of more directly personal instruments. 'To deny oneself, in order to follow Christ, to chastise the body, to hate one's own will. Not to seek after delicate living, not given to wine, not a glutton, not drowsy nor slothful, not to fulfil the desires of the flesh, but to love fasting, to love chastity.'

'To deny self': that is, the self which would be indulged, petted, yielded to, which has become like a sick person crying out for what would only make the illness worse; the self which must be denied or it will destroy itself. But there is a greater reason: 'in order to follow Christ'. The diseased, selfish self is to be made whole, not simply for our own good, but that we may present ourselves 'a living sacrifice, holy, acceptable unto God'; the self-loving servant restored to the service of the divine master.

A positive programme of self-discipline is set before us, with a definite end to be attained The body is to be chastised, not that it may be broken, but that it may be 'broken in' and become a willing servant of the soul. In what manner, and to what degree, depends upon each one's individual needs, and we may note how careful St Benedict is to avoid the excesses into which some of his predecessors had fallen. His directions about food and drink, clothes and sleep, notably his allowance of wine to his monks, probably scandalised many, in much the same way as many Anglo-Saxons are when they see monks smoking or having a pint of beer, a quite common sight in countries where, whatever their faults, hypocrisy is not among them.

'Not to seek after delicate living, or to become a winebibber or a glutton.' 'Not to seek'; that is the point. One need not fear to enjoy a good dinner, or a rare wine, when it is offered.

Excess is the sin. Overindulgence, whether in food or alcohol, is a sin of gluttony.

'Not drowsy or slothful' in habit, in the exercise of both our religious and common duties, but wide awake, alert, ready to repel an enemy or welcome a friend. And, in order that we may not 'fulfil the desires of the flesh', to love fasting, to love chastity; the former as a useful and at times necessary instrument, the latter for its own sake. Fasting does not occupy that place which it once did, and the church has modified its exercise even by monks. To go without food may not always be the best way of overcoming the 'sinful lusts of the flesh' in these days of tension, and of very different conditions of life from those of our forefathers. But the principle remains, and can be applied to what Shakespeare calls our 'pleasant vices'[67] by our keeping a guard on things lawful that so we are not led away by them. 'To love chastity' is another matter, and binding on all Christians, married or unmarried despite what the amoralist or the modern novelist thinks.

'Not a murmurer, not a detractor.' Murmuring in one's heart and under one's breath is a sin of the slothful, the envious, the comfort-loving, the discontented, of those who see everything in relation to themselves, and selfishly imagine that all should be as they desire it. Detraction consists in revealing the faults of others when there is no justification for doing so. That the facts are true is no excuse for broadcasting them, to the weakening or destroying of another's reputation. To do so is to sin against justice and charity.

Holy Scripture shows plainly that to love God and to love our neighbour are not two different things, but two facets of the same thing. In loving our neighbour we love God; in every sin against our neighbour we sin against God. 'Those who do not love a brother or sister, whom they have seen, cannot love God whom they have not seen.'[68]

Monday of the Fourth Week in Lent

What to fear, and what to hope for

The last Instruments of Good Works to be considered concern our personal and practical relation to the facts which our religion would have us treat as facts, and order our lives in view of them.

'To keep death daily before our eyes.' Does this mean we are to be always thinking of death? No; for at the moment we have even more important and factual things which need our attention, and upon which our future depends. But to see death as the inevitable thing it is, to get used to the idea of it as a reality which may at any moment overtake us, and so, treating it as a fact, to view it with calmness and live as those to whom its terrors are lightened by a right understanding of it as the passage to life eternal. The Archbishop of York, commenting upon our Lord's words, 'Very truly, I tell you, whoever keeps my word will never see death',[69] says that whilst this translation is correct it does obscure some of the meaning of the Greek, and offers in its place, 'If [you] observe my word, [you] shall not notice death unto eternity.' For our Lord is not promising exemption from 'the physical incident called death' but that if the mind is turned toward observing the word of Jesus 'death will be irrelevant to it'. We shall not notice it in the sense that one who had never perceived its true significance would.

'To fear the Day of judgement': and who must not do so who has any realisation of what God is and what we are? 'When the secrets of all hearts shall be revealed': the things we hid from ourselves, which we took no trouble to know, for which we had a thousand excuses. The moment of truth, of sight, of full understanding, which even the saints have feared, and taken care to anticipate by judging themselves ere came 'that day of wrath and mourning'. Let us reflect upon the fact that each day is a day of judgement, and that the day but confirms what already is. 'He that is unjust, let him be unjust still; and he that is filthy, let him be filthy still; and he that is righteous, let him be righteous still; and he that is holy, let him be holy still.'

'To be in dread of hell', of eternal separation from, and hatred toward, God and all good; the consummation of our own will, our own choice, a possibility which every choice of evil renders more possible.

'To desire with all spiritual longing everlasting life': not a mere endless continuance of life, but a new quality and fullness of life, a participation in the very eternity of God himself, in that divine life which is all delight and joy and love.

'To put one's hope in God': hope in which there is no shadow of doubt or misgiving, which relies on his mercy, his promises, and his power, which cannot, will not, ever disappoint us or let us down.

And, in that hope 'to apply oneself frequently to prayer', so sure a sign and reinforcement of our hope in God who alone can grant us grace in this life and glory in that which is to come.

'Daily to confess in prayer one's past sins, with tears and sighs to God, and to amend them for the future.'

'Not to wish to be called holy before one is so; but first to be holy, that one may be so called in truth.' For we must want to be saints, for to this are we called by God. 'You shall be holy, for I am holy.'[70] Very likely we do not think of ourselves as such; but how we purr like stroked cats when some foolish person tells us how good we are, and even in our denials have an ear open for a gentle insistence upon it!

And how are we to become holy? Whole, that is, with all our faculties and passions ordered and in their place, each contributing to a fuller, more integrated, harmonious, rightly directed life? By, says St Benedict, 'daily fulfilling by one's deeds the commandments of God'.

'And never to despair of the mercy of God.' We have been set a lifelong, difficult task, one which requires effort, attention, and constant perseverance. A task in which we fail again and again, sometimes deliberately, and often through our human frailty. The way is long, and often monotonous and tiring, and we are ever being tempted to exasperation with ourselves, to discouragement and despair, all of which is more harmful than the failures themselves. We mistake being sorry for ourselves for being sorry for our sins, and may even take pleasure in a morbid dwelling on our own misery. We forget that God would not allow us to fall into sins unless it were possible for us to derive good even from them, the good of an increased humility, a truer self-knowledge, a deeper penitence, a greater appreciation of the divine mercy. It is not our sins alone which displease him most, it is the slowness with which we return to him, our wallowing in the mud when we should be rising to throw ourselves at his feet in confident hope in his mercy.

Ever our pride and vanity rise to forget that, as Chesterton says, '[One] must love a thing very much if [one] not only practises it without any hope of fame or money, but even practises it without any hope of doing it well.' He is speaking of amateurs, and what else are we? If we love music, it is easy, but foolish, to get angry and discouraged because we cannot play the piano like Moiseivitch, who certainly only attained to that facility which delights us by endless practice and the solid determination to succeed. We cannot all be saints in the technical sense, any more than we can be great artists or musicians. But if we love God very much, we shall go on practising even without much 'hope of doing it well'. Anyway, we are not the judges of that; it would be a terrible thing if we came to think we were doing it well. The truly great are never satisfied with their attainment. And we need not worry about attaining, but only about desiring and doing our little best. The mercy of God will take care of the rest.

TUESDAY OF THE FOURTH WEEK IN LENT

With what are we to serve God – I

'For we must always serve him with the good things which he has given us.'

These words follow the injunction that in whatever good work we begin to do we should ask God 'with most earnest prayer to perfect it', and emphasise the fact that our good works have to be done with the 'good things which God has given us'. We might be inclined, at first, to think that the saint refers only to specifically 'spiritual' things, but if we read his words in the context of the whole of the Rule, we shall see that he includes all the good things, of nature as well as of grace, with which we have been endowed. For he has spoken already of the need of preparing not only our hearts but also our bodies for the service of God, and will legislate for manual labour as well as for worship, prayer, and study. And his outlook upon the common things which are necessary to daily life is shown in the directions as to the care with which the cellarer, who has charge of the material goods of the monastery, is to treat them: 'Let him look upon all the vessels and goods of the monastery as though they were the consecrated vessels of the altar. Let him not think that he may neglect anything.'

We can imagine, then, how St Benedict would have us regard and use that good thing which God has made our human soul-body nature, endowed with such splendid gifts, none of which may be neglected or made to serve any other master than he by whom and for whom we were created. Our Lord has made this plain in the parables of the talents and the pounds, and in such words as 'From everyone to whom much has been given, much will be required'.[71]

Whether our gifts be many or few, they carry with them the injunction, 'Trade until I come',[72] in that reckoning day when each servant shall be required to give an account of our stewardship.

The chief good of our human nature is the soul, so great a good that there can be but one answer to the question, 'What profit is there in gaining the whole world and losing one's own soul? or what shall one give in exchange for one's soul?' For the soul is one's very life, the source and principle of every activity, the seat of the image of God in which we were created, and of all those powers which raise us above the beasts of the field. Mind, will, imagination, memory, the passions, each is an activity of that spiritual, immortal self without which nothing is of any profit or use to us. The Faust legend tells us of one who sold his soul to the devil for the promise of a renewal of his physical life, a few more years of pleasure, the attainment of an earthly desire. We have not been so lost to our own good, but for what tiny things, for what useless and contemptible things, for what transient things, have we endangered our souls, risking our all as do gamblers in their folly, for what, when we grasped it, crumbled in our hands like Dead Sea fruit!

These good things of our nature, what have we done with them? Left them to rust unused, as so many do their thinking, reasoning faculties; abused them; turned them on unworthy objects; frittered them away in trivialities; failed, when it was necessary, to keep them in order, trained and disciplined for the service of God? Or have we forgotten that we are human beings and not angels, dreaming that we could live 'spiritual' lives in which nature had no real part to play? To attempt this is as harmful and unnatural as it is to attempt to live purely material lives. Grace requires nature; does not, in fact, exist apart from nature; is of no use to us save as it operates in and with nature. The good things of the supernatural order are given for the sake of those of the natural order, that human nature which God pronounced 'very good', and would restore and raise to a goodness above that which by sin it has lost. Grace is not a cloak with which we cover up our poverty and our wounds, it is that which removes the former and heals the latter. It is not merely a crutch by which, still lame, we manage to hobble along, but a rejuvenating remedy by which we are enabled, as was the lame beggar in the Temple porch, to leap up, stand, walk, and run 'praising God'.[73]

Christian asceticism and self-denial is not founded, as is that of Manicheism and Platonism, on the belief that the body and the passions are evil in themselves. On the contrary, it proceeds from, and is justified by, the belief that they are good with an inherent goodness which sin, however much it has weakened and injured, has not rendered incapable of restoration. That restoration cannot be effected without our own co-operation with the grace of God. The good which has gone wrong must be led back to its natural paths, the twisted mind and will made straight, the disordered passions subjected to the reign of reason and faith. And none of this is possible without self-discipline, self-control, self-denial, by which the whole of our nature is ordered aright, healed, and strengthened, that so all the resources of our being are brought into the service of God. Thus the good thing he made us is rescued from its enemies, enters into the 'glorious liberty of the children of God',[74] becomes a fighting unit in the holy war against the world, the flesh, and the devil, and reaches forward to that perfection which our divine master has bidden us seek, and the reward which he has promised to each good and faithful servant.

Wednesday of the Fourth Week in Lent

With what are we to serve God – II

'Serve him with the good things which he has given us.'

The good of our human nature depends upon, and is supported and perfected by, the good things around us, both of the natural and supernatural world. For 'the earth he has given to human beings',[75] or, as St Ignatius Loyola says, 'the other things on the face of the earth were created for [our] sake, and to help [us] in the seeking of the end for which [we were] created. Hence it follows that [we] should make use of creatures so far as they help [us] towards [our] end, and should abstain from them so far as they hinder [us] in regard of that end', which is 'to praise, reverence, and serve God, and by this means to save [our] soul'.

The goodness of the things of this world is witnessed to all through holy Scripture, and by the church in all ages, which has never yielded to the Manichean and Platonic heresy which holds that material things are evil in themselves. The fact that they were created by God, that they were made by and for his Word (as St Paul teaches) as also that by them humanity was meant to recognise the existence, power, and beauty of the eternal Godhead is sufficient evidence of their goodness and of the use to which they are to be put. Daily the church echoes the psalmist's praise of created things, the heavens which declare the glory of God, the firmament which shows his handiwork, the great, wide-flung waters of the ocean, the flowing stream, the rolling thunder, the high mountains, the tall cedars, the rain and snow and dew, the flames of fire, the corn and wine which make 'glad the human heart', the years crowned with the goodness of the Lord, the outgoings of the morning and evening which praise him, the beasts of the field and the birds of the air. 'O Lord, how manifold are your works! In wisdom you have made them all; the earth is full of your creatures.'[76] So, too, the church finds no better words with which to thank God for the highest of his gifts than those of the *Benedicite omnia opera*, which she puts upon the lips of her priests after Holy Communion.

But we must do more than this, we must use creatures in such a way as aids our service of God, as our Lord used them in his life on earth. For it is they, not merely the things of religion, such as prayer and sacraments, which are given to us to help us in reaching our end. We can no more live Christian lives without them than we can without the things of the spiritual order. 'One does not live by bread alone',[77] for we have a life which needs 'the bread that comes down from heaven';[78] but we cannot live without the necessities of our physical life. And if it is a crime to deprive people of the exercise of their religion, it is no less a crime, indeed a sin which cries out to God, to deprive people of their bodily needs.

To use or to abstain, this is the rule which is to govern our relation to created things. To use them in so far as they aid our service of God and advance us in the way of salvation. To use them with knowledge, with care and diligence; Christians ought not to need to be forced to a campaign against waste. We are stewards, not the owners, of the good things of this world for which we shall have to render an account.

To abstain from any good which, by our evil use of it, may become a hindrance to us in attaining our end. Note, from any good, not simply from such goods as beer, wine, tobacco, amusements, and the like. For it is not what we call 'bad' things which are our greatest danger, but good things, for these are most easily and commonly abused.

Beyond, yet inextricably mingled with, these good things of our nature and the universe are those of the supernatural order. The faith, the commandments, grace, sacraments, worship, prayer, fasting, almsgiving, the virtues, the gifts of the Holy Spirit, and all 'the riches of Christ', the inheritance of the children of God, these demand our understanding, careful, diligent, loving, and persevering use. For upon them depends not only the enlightening of our minds, that so we may see all things aright, but also the strengthening of our wills that we may choose and use all things as God wills, serving him with the good things of heaven, that, as St Benedict says, 'not only may he never, as an angry Father, disinherit his children, but may never, as a dread Lord, incensed by our sins, deliver us to everlasting punishment, as most wicked servants who would not follow him to glory.'

These are strong words of warning, but not one whit stronger than our Lord uses in the gospels about those who neglect or misuse the good things entrusted to them. Nor hardly comparable to those uttered by him who is 'the faithful and true witness' in the third chapter of the Apocalypse. 'I know your works; you are neither cold nor hot. I wish that you were either cold or hot',[79] for it is less to deny God than to believe in him yet treat him with contempt. 'So, because you are lukewarm, and neither cold nor hot, I am about to spit you out of my mouth. For you say, "I am rich, I have prospered, and I need nothing." You do not realise that you are wretched, pitiable, poor, blind, and naked',[80] destitute of that wedding garment of charity which in all humility begs of God, and uses, the good things he provides for them that love him.

Dear God, how good you are to me! Teach me to serve you as I ought.

The guidance of the Gospel

'Let us walk in his ways by the guidance of the Gospel.'

The whole purpose of the Christian religion is to show us the way of life, and to enable us to walk therein. Whilst it does give a design for living in this world, its gaze is fixed upon another world for which this life is but a preparation. It is not primarily concerned with morality and ethics, but with God; not with a Utopia of earth, nor with building 'Jerusalem in England's green and pleasant land', in the words of Blake's poem (which only gained notoriety from its association with a magnificent tune), but with 'Jerusalem which is above, mother of us all',[81] that city not 'made with hands, whose builder and maker is God'.[82]

To that city there is a way and ways, that way of him who said, 'I am the way',[83] the way promised of old, 'A highway shall be there, and it shall be called the Holy Way; the unclean shall not travel on it, but it shall be for God's people; no traveller, not even fools, shall go astray',[84] as did not those whom the Apostle names 'fools for Christ's sake'.[85] A way of holiness, to be trodden only by those who seek to become worthy of it. A way of security, in which the pilgrims of eternity, the wayfarers, may walk unafraid. A way marked out by him in whose steps we are called to tread, and in whose light we 'shall not walk in darkness, but shall have the light of life'.[86] A way not discovered by people, but revealed by God who, bidding us turn from our own ways and those of the world, says, 'This is the way, walk ye in it, and ye shall find rest for your souls.'[87]

There is but one way, but there are as many ways of walking in it as there are the particular vocations which God confers upon those who would serve him. Priest and laity, religious and secular, 'tinker, tailor, soldier, sailor', each has a particular way of praising, reverencing and serving God; each has a place in the long procession of pilgrims, the eyes of whose desire are strained to see 'the King in His beauty, and the land stretching very far off'.[88] So they walk, a motley throng, united in faith and hope and charity 'by the guidance of the gospel' which is their map, their chart, their guide to life eternal.

In speaking of the gospel St Benedict must not be understood to refer only to the four gospels, but to the whole of holy Scripture, in which 'the gospel of the blessed God' is gradually unfolded in order that we may become 'wise unto salvation through faith in Christ Jesus', with whom the whole of the sacred writings are concerned. For 'all scripture is inspired by God and is useful for teaching, for reproof, for correction, and for training in righteousness, so that everyone who belongs to God may be proficient, equipped for every good work'.[89] Nothing else can take the place which holy Scripture is meant to hold in the Christian life. The modern insistence upon the frequent reception of Holy Communion must not blind us to this fact, emphasised by spiritual guides in every age of the church. St Jerome says, 'To neglect the Scriptures is to neglect Christ,' and à Kempis, 'I acknowledge that I have need of two things, food and light. Therefore thou hast given me, weak as I am, thy sacred body for the nourishment of my soul and body, and thou hast set thy word as a lantern unto my feet. Without these two I could not well live, for the word of God is the light of my soul, and thy sacrament is the bread of life.'

We have spoken of holy Scripture as a map or chart, and this suggests the need of learning how to read it, just as one must learn to read a map or chart if they are to be of real use to us. To treat the Bible as any other book, to study it merely from the point of view of a critic or a historian, is to ignore the purpose for which it has been given which, in the words of St Thomas, is 'to bind the soul to God, the living and true'. What we are to look for above everything else is what God thinks and reveals of himself and of his creation, and of humanity his children; what he wills for, and desires of us; what he commands; what he has done for us and has promised to do for those who would know, love, and serve him.

There is no better corrective for the false teaching, the unworthy conceptions of God, the wrong ideas and impressions, the ignorance displayed in much modern writing about the meaning of life in general or of the Christian religion in particular, than such a reading of Scripture will give us. For therein the Truth himself speaks 'in many ways',[90] first through the halting lips of the teachers, prophets, and psalmists of old time in most sure words. St Peter says of scripture, 'You will do well to be attentive to this as to a lamp shining in a dark place, until the day dawns,'[91] and the full word is plainly uttered in God's Son by whom, as St John of the Cross writes, 'He has spoken to us altogether, once and for all, in this single Word, and he has no more to say . . . Set thine eyes on him alone.' We might well hear God say to us, 'for in him have I spoken and revealed all things to thee, and in him thou shalt find yet more than that which thou desirest and askest,' for in Christ 'I have spoken to thee, answered thee, declared and revealed to thee, in giving him to thee, as thy brother, companion, and master, as ransom and reward.' 'This is my beloved Son, hear him.'[92]

Let us confess, with St Peter, 'You alone have the words of eternal life';[93] with Magdalene sit at Jesus' feet and listen to his words; with our Lady keep and ponder them in our hearts (for has he not said, 'Blessed are they who hear the word of God and keep it'?[94]), receiving the seed of the divine word in the good ground of a humble and loving heart, that so it may bring forth fruit a hundredfold.

Friday of the Fourth Week in Lent

Stability and perseverance

The final words of the Prologue to the Holy Rule, 'So that never departing from his guidance, but persevering in his teaching in the monastery until death', express the essential vow of the Benedictine, which is that of stability. Unlike the members of many other religious orders, he does not so much join a society in which he may be transferred from one house to another, but a family, largely autonomous in character, and confined to the particular monastery in which he makes his vows. Here, in a very special sense, is his home, his father, his brethren; here the particular application of the Rule which, according to various circumstances, differs from one house to another.

This vow of stability, so understood, concerns the monk alone, but the spirit of it concerns each Christian who, in baptism, is made a member of the body of Christ, the household of God, the catholic church, of which we say with the psalmist, 'This shall be my rest for ever, here will I dwell, for I have a delight therein.' The church is his home, his Father's house, wherein he is to abide, never departing from God's guidance, but persevering in his teaching until death. For stability and perseverance are the most necessary things in the Christian life. 'The one who endures to the end will be saved,'[95] says our Lord.

There is a French proverb, *Ce n'est que le premier pas qui coûte* – it is the first step which costs – and, no doubt, there is some truth in this, for the first step often requires an effort, as St Benedict sees clearly. But it is not the whole truth, for the really costing thing is the going on to the end. We can remember how easily and gladly we took the first step of a summer day's walk, or perhaps of the ascent of a mountain, little thinking of the costing efforts which would have to be made later on. And in Christians, says St Jerome, 'it is not the beginning but the end which is required'.

'Never to depart' from the church, for '[one] who has not the church for [a] mother cannot have God for [a] Father', writes St Augustine, and, 'Outside the church there is no salvation'. In the first chapter of the Holy Rule St Benedict speaks of four classes of monks: the Cenobites, 'who do their service in a monastery, under a rule and an abbot'; the Hermits, who, having been well tried, go forth to the single-handed combat of the desert; the Sarabaites, who having never submitted to any rule, nor been 'tried by experience . . . make a law to themselves of their own pleasures and desires; doing whatever they think fit, or what pleases them, and calling it holy'; and the Gyrovagues, 'who spend all their lives wandering about, ever roaming, with no stability . . . of whose wretched life it is better to say nothing than to speak'.

It is not difficult to see that there are Christians living in the world who correspond to the first and the last two of these classes. There are those who live in the Lord's house in faith and obedience to his commands, living by rule, ordering their lives by the precepts of his church. There are those who have no rule, nor any real experience of what it is to be a Christian, whose life is governed by self-pleasing, who choose what of Christian faith and practice is agreeable to them, believing and doing what they think fit, substituting a religion of their own contriving for that of Jesus Christ and his church. And there are those who are forever wandering about from one form of religion to another, 'taking up' first this cult and then that, those well described by the Apostle, who 'will not put up with sound doctrine, but having itching ears . . . will accumulate for themselves teachers to suit their own desires, and will turn away from listening to the truth and wander away to myths'.[96] The world is as full of 'false prophets' today as ever it was.

If the Christian life is to be stable and persevering, it must be built on that rock which is Christ, the incarnate God, and abide in the faith which derives from his person and teaching. For there alone it comes into contact with, touches, and is made one with, reality; is born of, and feeds on, the supreme truth, the 'common Good', as Aquinas calls God, the Good of everyone; drinks of the living water of eternal life. Our faith and practice must be one of conviction not of mere acquiescence; founded, not on any human word, on feeling and sentiment, or even on any experience, real or imaginary, we may have had, but solely on God's word, revealed to us in and by Jesus Christ, 'in whom are all the treasures of wisdom and knowledge', who is 'the way, the truth, and the life'. The divine-human way by which we are to walk; the divine truth expressed in human form, translated into the terms of our human language, that all who read may run surely and safely toward the end for which they were created; the divine life, of which we are made partakers, that we may live as new creatures, since, as Origen wrote in the second century, 'From Jesus there began the interweaving of the divine and human natures, in order that the human, by communion with the divine, might rise to be divine; not in Jesus alone, but in all those who not only believe but enter upon the life which Jesus taught'.

Worship

The Holy Rule makes the Benedictine day revolve round three comprehensive activities: worship, study, and work, the last term being applied chiefly to manual labour, though this is often superseded nowadays by teaching, parish work and similar occupations. In St Benedict's day, and for some centuries later, monasteries were self-contained and self-supporting, having their own farms, workshops, etc., as well as schools and the spiritual care of the faithful in the neighbourhood. Modern conditions have changed this in most cases, and the actual manual labour which remains is often done by lay brothers. But to St Benedict manual labour is but one form of work, and for the monk the recitation of the divine Office is the *opus Dei*, of which he says, 'Let nothing be put before the work of God', and to the ordering of which he devotes sixteen of the seventy-three chapters of the Rule. Some readers may be surprised that, although he mentions Mass several times, taking it, as he does many other things, as a matter of course, he does not legislate for it. And rightly, for the ordering of Mass is not committed to individuals, but to the church, so that whilst the Benedictine Office varies from that recited by secular priests, the Mass is that common to the Roman Church.

As we are writing for Christians who have no obligation to recite the divine Office, we shall refer only to what the saint has to say about worship in general, and to some implications of his teaching. Worship is the chief act of religion, which itself is one manifestation of the virtue of justice, a point to be emphasised in our day when it is too often regarded, not as an obligation, a necessary Christian duty, but as an act left to the choice of, and dictated by the variable feelings of, the individual. An act, too, which is deemed to fulfil its purpose only when worshippers derive, or imagine that they have derived, some good from it. All this is contrary to the whole meaning of Christian worship, which is not derived from the inclination or feelings of the individual but from what, in justice, humanity owes to God.

To many non Roman Catholics, and most non Christians, the idea that to miss Mass wilfully on a Sunday or day of obligation is to sin even more seriously than in not paying one's debts or acting unjustly in any other way seems almost absurd. Yet must one act justly to one's neighbour and not to God? Is it to him alone that we owe nothing? Must we obey the state, our parents, our employers, whether we feel like it or not, but obey God only when we like or because we get some benefit from so doing?

Worship is an act by which we render to God that which he justly deserves because he is God. If we are to derive good from it, then it must be such worship as is worthy of him to whom it is offered, and so is nothing less than an entire offering of oneself to God. Strictly speaking, there is but one worship and one worshipper, Jesus Christ, for he alone is capable of offering, and has actually offered, a worship commensurate with the divine majesty. It is not as a solitary individual but as a 'member of Christ' that the Christian is enabled to worship 'in spirit and in truth', whether primarily in taking part in the act in which the church obeys the command, 'Do this, in remembrance of me', or in such other acts as the church has always grouped round the worship of Mass, the chief of which are the seven canonical hours of the divine Office.

In the chapter entitled, 'How to Say the Divine Office', St Benedict is concerned with corporate worship, and recurs to his oft-repeated belief 'that the divine presence is everywhere . . . but especially, without any doubt, when we are assisting at the divine work. Let us, then, ever remember what the prophet says, “Serve the Lord in fear”; and again, “Sing praises with understanding”; and, “In the presence of the angels will I sing praise to you.” Therefore, let us consider how we ought to behave in the presence of God and of his angels, and so assist at the divine Office, that mind and voice be in harmony.’ Elsewhere he speaks of those who may be working too far away from the monastery to return at the appointed hour at which the Office is recited, and of those who are journeying, and orders that the former ‘shall perform the work of God where they are, bending their knees in godly fear’, and that the latter are not ‘to neglect to pay their due of service’. Punishment is to be meted out to those who come late or who make mistakes in reciting any part of the Office.

To St Benedict worship is a work, the *opus Dei*, which, demands the utmost attention, reverence, awe and understanding that can be given to it. We need not, then, be surprised to find it difficult, demanding, and, at times, tiring. Much of the poverty of our worship arises from our not understanding this, and so assuming that it can be performed easily without much real effort of mind or will, as one plays a game of tennis just for fun, not in the strenuous ways of Wimbledon. We expect to be interested, pleased, gratified, set at ease, comforted – and what has any of this to do with the worship of God? If we get little or no good it is because we have given little or nothing, have done no work, rendered no service. We criticise the priest, the choir and organist, other members of the congregation, any one but ourselves who need it most, and even complain that God has neglected us, when we might well rather be thankful that he has overlooked our impertinence.

Worship is a sacrificial work; let us remember that, and see to it that there is sacrifice and service in our worship, a cheerful giving of what God expects of us, a sharing in that worship which found its culminating expression upon Calvary, at which the chief assistants were a mother whose heart was pierced with a sword of sorrow, a disciple who had learnt what love really meant and entailed, and a penitent sinner who from the worship of self-pleasing had been brought to the worship of the Lord who 'pleased not himself'.

Passion Sunday

Prayer

The object of the Holy Rule being to order the lives and actions of men and women who, as religious, live in community, it is not surprising to find very little which has to do with the private observances and practices of the Christian life. There is, for example, very little about private prayer, though undoubtedly much instruction would be given upon this, and other matters, in conferences and sermons. The nature of such teaching may be gathered from the last chapter, in which St Benedict speaks of the Rule as a guide to 'a beginning of religious life', and goes on to say that those who would hasten to its perfection will find all they need in holy Scripture, 'a most accurate rule for human life'; and in the books of the holy Catholic fathers, of which he mentions the Conferences of Cassian, the Institutes of the same author, the Lives of the Fathers, and 'the Rule of our holy Father Basil'. These were amongst the chief 'spiritual' books of his time (as, indeed, holy Scripture must ever be), and if, since then, they have been added to and multiplied, they still remain the source of the soundest teaching upon the Christian life.

The chapter on reverence at prayer is short but very instructive. 'If, when we wish to make any request to people in power, we presume not to do so except with humility and respect, how much more ought we with all lowliness and purity of devotion to make our supplications to the Lord God? And let us remember that we are not heard for our much speaking, but for our purity of heart and tears of compunction shall we be heard. Therefore, prayer ought to be short and pure, except, perchance, it be prolonged by the inspiration of divine grace. But let prayer made in common always be short.' And in the chapter on the Oratory he directs that when the Office is ended all should leave 'with the utmost silence, and let reverence be paid to God'; so that any one who wishes to pray alone may not be disturbed. 'But if any one wishes to pray by himself, let him go in with simplicity and pray, not with a loud voice, but with tears and fervour of heart.'

Notice, first, the saint's direction that prayer, whether in common or private, should be short, for what was short to him may well seem long to us. The day offices are comparatively short, but the night office of Matins and Lauds might take a couple of hours or more, and was to be followed by spiritual reading and meditation until Prime at daybreak, after which Mass would be said. Therefore, when he says that private prayer should be short, it is in comparison with the corporate prayer of the monastery, and must not be taken to mean 'short' in the sense we should probably use the term.

More important, of course, are the conditions which St Benedict lays down for private prayer. It must be humble, reverent, pure (he uses the word three times – 'pure', 'purity of devotion', 'purity of heart'), full of compunction, but with few words, offered with simplicity and fervour of heart. Here, indeed, is a great deal in a few words. Prayer is to be humble, for 'the prayer of the humble pierceth the skies', and is heard by him who is with all that are humble and contrite of spirit; reverent in spirit and posture, pure in intention, in devotion, in singleness of heart. Wholly given to what is being done: the act of one who does not merely feel some sensible devotion, but is devoted to the will of God which prayer does not seek to change but to know and fulfil. Full of compunction ('a broken heart, O God, you will not despise'[97]), which may be manifested outwardly with tears, but must be ever present inwardly. The expression 'tears of compunction' is Cassian's, who, relating the Conferences of the Abbot Isaac, tells how he spoke of the various sentiments which evoked compunction within the heart – the remembrance of our sins, the fear of judgement and of hell, the consideration of the joy of heaven, for one may weep for very joy as well as for sadness, or that sorrow of heart caused by the sins of others, as when Jesus wept over the holy city.

'But with few words', for, as says the Preacher, 'God is in heaven and thou on earth', therefore, ' remembering that he is all and thou art nothing, let thy words be few'. Or, as our Lord has told us, we are not heard for our much speaking. But who, looking at our manifold intercession lists and forms of prayer would believe it? One would imagine that we thought that God needed to be informed of what was happening in his world, and that we were his Ministry of Information. Or that we must be constantly finding more words in which to express our needs, when it might be said more truly that God can hardly hear us because of the chattering we indulge in at our prayers.

Prayer should become more simple, not more diffuse and complicated. 'If any one wants to pray, let him go in with simplicity and pray.' Theory is good, but to know the theory of prayer alone will not enable us to pray; we must practise, just as no amount of the theory of music will enable us to play a piano or violin without practice. We can learn to pray only by praying, and the simpler our prayer the better it will be. 'Think of the Lord with a good heart, and in simplicity of heart seek him,' says the book of Proverbs

'With fervour of heart.' True fervour is not a feeling of the senses but a stable, unremittent attitude of the will set on seeking God. It does not go by fits and starts, at times driving us to worship and prayer, at others leaving us careless and neglectful of our Christian duties. Fervour is most fervour when we do not want to pray, find it difficult and dry, yet go on praying, if only to remain before God, waiting upon him, longing for him, desiring him. It is one example of 'indifference' as St Ignatius uses the term, having no choices, accepting the state of prayer which God wills, remaining steady and constant, moderate and discreet, whether in times of sensible devotion or when no such evanescent flame fires our purpose. By it we become praying people, not just people who say prayers, but praying always, which for the greater part of our time means desiring and doing the will of God.

Monday in Passiontide

Study

Study, in the commonly accepted meaning of the word, can be but the occupation of the minority of people, although it is surprising to find how much time and energy any one who is interested in a particular subject can and does find to devote to it. The people who complain that they have no time for some form of study are not usually those who are actually living busy lives, but those who fritter away their time in more or less useless pursuits, or live such ill-regulated lives that, as they say, they have no time for anything.

St Benedict is, of course, mainly concerned with such studies as befit the religious life, but from the first Benedictines did not confine themselves to specifically 'religious' subjects. It was a Benedictine monk, St Bede, who wrote the first history of England, and it is to Benedictines that we owe the preservation of learning, in all its branches, during and after the Dark Ages. No one would claim that all Christians should study in the ordinary sense of the word, but Christians who do not give some time and thought to divine things (of which they make profession that they excel all others in importance) can hardly be taken to mean what they say. For all people do think about, and desire to know more of, any subjects which interest them, and if Christians are not interested in the things of their religion they have not more claim to the name than is theirs by the fact of their baptism.

The word St Benedict uses for study is 'meditation,' which is derived from *meditor*, the primary meaning of which is to practise, to exercise oneself in some way, to act, and thus came to be applied to the act of studying, or meditating upon, some subject or purpose, in order to carry it out in the best possible manner. And that is the sense in which the saint uses the word when he lays down that after the recitation of the Night Office the brethren must study those parts of the Psalter and Lessons which they have still to learn, that so they may take their part in the Office well and intelligently. In later chapters he uses the word 'reading', to which each is 'to devote himself', and also the word 'meditate', as when he says, 'If any one be so negligent and slothful as to be unwilling or unable to read or meditate, let [them] be given some work that [they] be not idle.'

Spiritual reading and meditation (which is nothing else but thinking about what we read, with a view to such action as it implies) are insisted upon by all the guides of the Christian life. It is not so much a question of what amount of time can be spent, but the amount of thought which ought to be given to divine things. There is no real excuse for the ignorance which large numbers of Christians seem to regard almost as a virtue, especially as this is so largely true of those who have had educational advantages, and have a certain amount of leisure. 'He was brought up to believe in God, but not to think of him,' says Somerset Maugham of one of his characters, and how true this is of thousands who reserve all their thinking for mundane affairs, and even resent being told that they should think about God and divine things. The result is seen both in the little influence their belief has upon their lives (for how can that influence us which we do not think about?) and in the false, inadequate, and superstitious ideas of God which are so common; and which one would scarcely believe to be possible after twenty centuries of Christianity, were they not so naïvely repeated.

It is unfortunate that the term 'meditation' has come to be almost exclusively applied to some method of mental prayer, since this gives rise both to the idea that meditation is prayer, instead of being only a preparation for prayer, and to the saying 'I cannot meditate', which on inquiry is found to mean, not 'I cannot think', but, 'I cannot pray according to a method of mental prayer'. This may be so, either because one has never been taught or because one has passed beyond this stage of prayer. But, whichever be true, one can think, use one's reason, upon divine things, so that what is real and actual may become real and actual to oneself. Such thinking is necessary, not only that we may come to know the things of God, but also that we may have a right judgement in all things and not be like Lucinda Pasqueral-Montagu who 'accepted and observed all the practices of religion' without 'thinking religiously'. It is a nice phrase, and must not be interpreted to mean thinking piously, but in the light of divine and eternal realities to think rightly, rationally, Christianly, about all things. It is to have a standard by which we estimate and value people and things, a standard other than that of the world and the spirit of the times.

The apostle reminds us also that our thinking need not, indeed must not, be confined to the things of religion, but should extend to whatever is true, honest, just, pure, lovely, and of good report, and this may well be remembered by those who think it necessary to restrict their reading and thinking to what are known as 'spiritual' books. For it is possible to have too much of a good thing, as both the proverb and experience show. Von Hugel was right when he insisted upon the need of 'non religious interests', saying that without some such interest 'religion itself grows thin and poor, sentimental', of little use to the one who indulges in it, and more harm than good to every one else.

To try and live the Christian life in the world on a diet of 'pious' books, and the more sensational daily newspapers and periodicals, as some do, is as foolish as to attempt to live on confectionery and cheap champagne. Not from the clergy alone, but from every Christian, according to ability and circumstances, a devotion to truth is required, a use of those mental faculties which are not given merely for the rational consideration of the things of this life, but whose supreme need is to be found in the pursuit of that knowledge of God which our Lord declares to be eternal life.

Tuesday in Passiontide

Work

'Idleness is the enemy of the soul. Therefore should the brethren be occupied at stated times in manual labour, and at other fixed hours in sacred reading.' These words begin the chapter on the daily manual labour of the monk, but in it we find matter relating to the use of the whole time outside that spent in reciting the divine Office, hearing Mass and so on. It may be regarded, therefore, as a chapter on the right use of our time, of which St Benedict has spoken so movingly in the Prologue to the Rule. 'If we would arrive at eternal life, escaping the pains of hell, then, while there is yet time, while we are still in the flesh, and are able to fulfil all these things by the light which is given us, we must hasten to do what will profit us for all eternity.' Has not our Lord bidden us, 'Work while it is yet day, for the night is coming when no one can work';[98] when 'time shall be no more', and nought but what we have done with shall remain? 'My times are in your hand,'[99] says the psalmist, and, 'Remember how short my time is.'[100] But our time, like our lives, is also in our own hands, an incredibly precious possession, in the moments of which we are weaving out either a patchwork of bits and ends according to our own fancy, or a pattern of which the model has been given in the divine-human life of Jesus; the materials lie around us, and the power to use them flows from the inexhaustible source of the grace of God.

By a fortunate disposition of the divine Providence most people have very little time in which to be idle. The necessities of life enclose them in a rule as demanding as that which governs the time of a monk, and frequently much less profitable. Let us not talk glibly about the 'dignity of labour', for whilst there is labour which dignifies the one who performs it, much labour of our time has little of dignity about it. To sweep a street, to labour on the land, the labour of the scientist, of those who actually make things with their hands, or design them with their minds, all this may, and should, dignify a person. But to sit for hours monotonously attending to the gadget of a machine which turns out some article in the actual production of which no thought or skill is required, but only an automatic, machine-like precision, as of a robot, requires some stretch of imagination to merit the name. It can, indeed, only do so when the result is worthy of the effort, mechanical as it may be, and this is far from being the case with a large number of things which such labour is concerned in producing, neither for beauty nor service but simply to enrich the few who trade upon the foolishness and gullibility of their fellows. Such labour has such a demonising effect that it can be only compared with idleness as one evil is to another, its only value being in that people are paid for doing it and thus enabled, if they will, to use what time is left to them in ways which contribute to life as it is meant to be.

What is idleness? Not simply to do nothing, which in fact is impossible, since there is always some activity, if not of the body, yet of the mind, going on. Nor the idling of a holiday spent, perchance, in lying on the seashore, or upon a hillside just resting in an enjoyment of freedom from work or care. But wasting our time, as spendthrifts waste their money and are astonished when they find it is gone beyond recall. Spending our time on worthless objects and pursuits which often have no other purpose than 'to pass away the time', as those do who, to their misery, have nothing better to occupy their time than in gossiping, looking in shop windows, playing bridge all day, going from one cinema to another on almost every day of the week, drifting from house to house, from pleasure to pleasure, or living in the past or the future, while the present, the only time they have, is neglected and lost. Procrastinating, dawdling, frittering away precious moments, 'living and scarcely living' in daydreams and castles in the air, without order, rule and discipline; anaemic, mediocre, purposeless lives, such are they who by idleness betray themselves to this potent enemy of their souls.

What we have said so far concerns common forms of idleness which corrode and injure human lives. There is another kind, which we may call 'spiritual idleness' in Christians who would not give place to those already mentioned, and is usually known as 'slothfulness' which the church teaches is a deadly sin. One of its chief characteristics is putting off duties which should be performed, so that they, not being done at the proper time, accumulate, become burdensome, and are either left undone or done hastily and perfunctorily. Another is the habit of being about to do something which is necessary, yet not beginning to do it. Not rising at a given time in order that we may begin the day calmly in the remembered presence of God is another. Slothfulness is shown also in making resolutions and not keeping them; in not attending to inspirations which the Holy Spirit gives to us; in carelessness and slovenliness at worship, in prayer, and in receiving sacraments; in talking too much, especially about our spiritual life; in reading many spiritual books without any real attention, or intention of putting into practice what is fitting to our particular needs and vocation.

All this waste of time breeds dullness of spirit, often disguised under a multiplicity of 'good works' which are little worth since they proceed from a desire to escape from more necessary duties; a growing lukewarmness, and consequent impatience with the demands of worship, prayer, and self-discipline, and a general sense of unreality with regard to divine things.

In former days, when a person became alive to the seriousness, the urgency, and the demands of the Christian life, the first thing that happened was not merely a stricter attention to worship, prayer, mortification and the like, but also the seeking of ways in which to perform the corporal works of mercy. Inspired by the love of Christ, Christians gave themselves to a very practical love of their neighbour, devoting the time once spent in useless occupations to tending the sick, aiding the poor, visiting prisoners, redeeming captives, burying the dead. Now that the state has taken over these activities, such opportunities have become fewer, and it is more difficult to do such good works in person. But Christians could do more than they often do, in arousing the conscience of the public in the matter of social and economic evils which still exist, without waiting to be driven to seek remedies for them by the catastrophe of war.

But first the enemy of idleness must be driven out of our own lives, and for this we must live by rule, order our time and our occupations so far as they lie in our power, and so give value to each present moment, for on this 'Now' all else depends.

Zeal, good and bad

All through the Holy Rule we find the complementary virtues of zeal and discretion which occupy so marked a place in the life and character of St Benedict. His whole mind is set upon the glory of God and the salvation of souls, with an intensity of zeal which, at the same time, is tempered to human frailty and needs by a discretion and moderation which has not always characterised the zealous for God. And this is due partly to the fact that he knew by experience that 'there is an evil zeal of bitterness which separates from God, and leads to hell', as well as 'a good zeal, which separates from vices and leads to God and everlasting life. Let monks, then, practise this zeal with most fervent love, that is, in honour, preventing one another. Let them most patiently endure one another's infirmities, whether of body or character. Let them obey one another with rivalry. Let no one follow what he judges good for himself, but rather what seems good for another. Let them exercise the charity of brotherhood with chaste love. Let them fear God; love their abbot with sincere and humble affection; and prefer nothing to Christ'. What could be more simply Christian, tend more to the peace of households, society, and the church, of the members of which it was once said, 'See how these Christians love one another'? For how shall peace reign except where people of goodwill show zealous charity one to another?

'There is an evil zeal', of which St James speaks: 'But if you have bitter envy and selfish ambition in your hearts, do not be boastful and false to the truth. Such wisdom does not come down from above, but is earthly, unspiritual, devilish. For where there is envy and selfish ambition, there will also be disorder and wickedness of every kind.'[101] The zeal of the Pharisee, of the 'unco'guid', the self-righteous, the inquisitor, the contentious, the controversialist, the rigorist, the impatient, destroying the very good they are seeking to uphold, and defend.'[102] 'The Lord's servant must not be quarrelsome,' the Apostle admonishes St Timothy, 'but kindly to everyone, an apt teacher, patient, correcting opponents with gentleness.'

'And there is a good zeal' born of charity, and of 'the wisdom that comes down from above', a zeal manifested in love and patience, in honouring one another, in courtesy and forbearance, in enduring the infirmities of others, whether of body or character, in being more ready to obey than to command, in considering the good of others before our own, in all things preferring nothing to Christ. Every chapter of the Rule which has to do with those who are placed in positions of authority contains some reference to this good zeal, for St Benedict knew well what a dangerous thing authority and power can become in the hands of frail men and women. It is altogether right that we should be zealous for truth, for the exercise of any office we may be called to occupy, for seeing that respect and obedience are given by those from whom it is due. But more important still is the manner and spirit in which we exercise our zeal which must be that of him who was consumed by zeal for his Father's house, yet would not break the bruised reed, nor quench the still smoking flax, and whose tender, patient, enduring courtesy is to be our model.

Zeal must ever be tempered by charity, and charity demands discretion, which, it is said, St Antony claimed was the highest of the virtues since it moderated all the rest. It is true, as says St Bernard, that 'the measure of loving God is to love him without measure', but when we come to the practical expression of our love for God, discretion will teach us that it has to be measured by many things. We may attempt to do too much, or what is not consonant with our vocation or our grace. We may, as some of the saints discovered, harm our minds or our bodies by indiscreet mortifications, overburden ourselves with practices which we find we cannot keep up, read too many spiritual books, indulge in too much churchgoing, so that presently we get tired of them, be too intense in prayer and receiving the sacraments, so that we suffer from fatigue and become irritable and unbearable.

In fact there are few if any of us who do not need discretion in most of our daily actions and words, for example in such common things as eating and drinking, the clothes we wear, the ordering of our time, our dealings with others, our recreations, our giving and receiving of advice, the outward expression of our faith, the direction of those under our authority, the art of dealing with different people, and not least of knowing when to see and when not to see what is going on around us; on most of which things St Benedict has something to say.

Yet let it not be forgotten (especially by those who, on reading the above, might be inclined to say, 'I told you so,' and congratulate themselves on the imagined discretion with which they manage to do so little for God) that it is difficult to distinguish them from those who make no pretence of doing anything save for themselves. For discretion would have us aim at an approach to the maximum, not to be content with the bare minimum. Most of us are more tempted to do too little than too much, and may need to be reminded that meanness is not a virtue pleasing to God any more than it is praised by people. To be discreet and prudent is not to sit down in the spiritual life – which indeed is impossible since if we are not going forward, however slowly and perchance cautiously, we shall be going back.

Discretion will cause us to act slowly and quietly, not on impulse and sentiment but guided by reason and faith; to do what lies within our strength, however little, but to do it well and perseveringly, will enable us to see what and how to add from time to time, and what to leave behind; teach us to walk before we attempt to run; sink us deeper in humility, in confidence in God as a strong balance to mistrust of self; will save us from making vices of our virtues and keep us in the way and at the place where God daily looks for us. For it is the companion of those who persevere to the end.

Thursday in Passiontide

Humility – I

[This section on humility has been very substantially edited. Today's understanding of the human psyche makes it even more necessary to distinguish between humility and negative self-deprecation; between healthy self-esteem and sinful pride. In some cases, this has necessitated the insertion of complete paragraphs which, while still being faithful to the Rule, reflect the editor's, rather than the author's particular outlook. These paragraphs are distinguished from the original text by being indented and bracketed as this one.]

It is fitting that as we draw near to Palm Sunday, the Collect for which speaks of the 'tender love' of God 'towards mankind', and of the humility and patience of our Lord, we should consider those sayings of St Benedict which concern our following of our divine master in such manner as will enable us to 'be made partakers of his resurrection'.

Chapter seven of the Rule is devoted to the subject of humility, the necessity of which St Benedict founds on the teaching of holy Scripture, thus making it plain that whilst some of the external expression of this virtue is peculiar to religious, the interior spirit is necessary for all Christian life: 'The holy Scripture cries out to us, saying, "All who exalt themselves will be humbled, and all who humble themselves will be exalted."[103] In saying this it teaches us that all exaltation is a kind of pride, against which the psalmist shows himself to be on his guard when he says, "O Lord, my heart is not lifted up, my eyes are not raised too high; I do not occupy myself with things too great and too marvellous for me."[104] And why? "I have calmed and quieted my soul, like a weaned child with its mother; my soul is like the weaned child that is with me."'[105]

He goes on to speak of 'the humility of our present life' by which we erect a ladder 'of our ever-ascending actions' by which, 'if the heart be humbled', our life 'is lifted up by the Lord to heaven'. The sides of this ladder are 'our body and soul, in which the call of God has placed various degrees of humility, or discipline, which we must ascend'.

Before we consider these degrees, let us mark clearly what Christian humility is. Negatively, it is the opposite, the contrary, the negation, of pride and vanity and vainglory. Positively, it is the recognition, and acknowledgement of the truth about oneself. 'Humility,' writes Père Lacordaire in his *Letters to Young Men*, 'does not consist in hiding our talents and virtues, in thinking ourselves worse and more ordinary than we are, but in possessing a clear knowledge of all that is lacking in us, and in not exalting ourselves for that which we have, seeing that God has freely given it to us.' The distinction is important, for there is a spurious humility which manifests itself in a self-deprecation which, born of pride, seeks only to be contradicted and praised. Many a 'I know I'm no good' is simply asking to be told 'But, of course you are', as is 'I don't pretend to be a saint', which awaits the enumeration of one's virtues from an admiring friend.

Humility is a true estimation of one's worth. We often hear the question, 'What is So-and-so worth?' The answers will vary, but seldom, if ever, do we hear the really true one, that people are worth what they are in the sight of God. To gain some sight of that worth is the foundation of humility. For what is the measure of our worth to God? How foolish is all our pride, our glorying in ourselves and our achievements, our childish vanity, our pretensions, our assumptions that such things as money, possessions, talents, and so on confer some intrinsic worth upon us which even God ought to recognise! One of the great hallmarks of saints is their ability to take a true, sensible, rational view of themselves, and so be saved from the foolishness, the vulgarity, the strutting absurdities of the proud and vain, whose very seriousness adds to the ludicrous character of their words and deeds.

> [A true estimation of one's worth, of what one is to God, is very different both from self-exalting conceit and the negative self-deprecation, even self-loathing which too many people have been encouraged to think of as a virtue. Our worth in the sight of God is shown by two essential statements: that God made us in his image and that in Christ he became human and died for us. To be created in God's image, and for him to become human, means that humanity is essentially good; his dying for us indicates the seriousness of our fallen, sinful condition at the same time as affirming beyond any doubt that he loves us infinitely and eternally, and desires nothing but our salvation. To such a God we come not as worthy, deserving people, but as sinners saved by grace – but who *are* saved and who *are* worth saving. Such an understanding should save us from the extreme poles of self-loathing and self-exaltation.]

All self-exaltation is a kind of pride; it is not a prerogative of the rich or those in high position. People from all walks of life can be equally guilty of such things as neglect of God, snobbishness and self-opinionatedness. And Christians are the worst examples, since they, of all people, ought – and profess – to know better. One would have thought that the pharisaic spirit was sufficiently exposed and condemned in the New Testament to render it impossible to a Christian were it not so obvious in many who seem to have learnt nothing from the humility of the Lord, nor regard his words: 'For I tell you, unless your righteousness exceeds that of the Scribes and Pharisees, you will never enter the kingdom of heaven.'[106]

Humility demands self-knowledge, the knowledge of one's place in the sight of God, of one's sins – which are born of pride, of that vanity which, like the flaunting of a peacock, preens itself before the aweful majesty of the Creator, and in attributing one's good entirely to oneself, robs God of the praise which is due to him. And no less knowledge of God, for if that were what it ought to be, who would play the fool before him, and not rather cry with the prophet, 'Woe is me! I am lost, for I am a man of unclean lips, and I live among a people of unclean lips; yet my eyes have seen the King, the Lord of hosts.'[107] Or with Job, 'I had heard of you by the hearing of the ear, but now my eye sees you. Therefore I despise myself, and repent in dust and ashes.'[108] How much more shall we who in Passiontide see the humility of God-made-man who 'humbled himself and became obedient to the point of death',[109] leaving us an example in the act by which he made it possible for us 'to follow in his steps'.[110]

Friday in Passiontide

Humility – II

'The first degree of humility is that [one] always keep the fear of God before [one's] eyes, avoiding all forgetfulness.'

St Benedict has spoken already, as he does constantly throughout the Rule, of the remembrance and fear of God which is the beginning of that wisdom by which we forsake the sloth of disobedience to set out upon the way of the service of God.

[In modern usage, we rightly question the word 'fear' and prefer to replace it with 'respect' or 'awe'. Clearly, God no more wants his children to live in fear of him than does any good human parent, and yet we need to avoid the opposite error of thinking of God as an *indulgent* parent to the extent that any such awe in his presence becomes mere sentimentality. To this end, the proper use of the word 'fear' may be a helpful corrective.]

'Always.' The fact of God, of his universal presence, that, as the saint adds, we should consider that all we do is done in that presence and we should no more dishonour God by unseemly conduct in front of him than we would any person in whose company we found ourselves and whose goodwill we valued. And not only our actions but our thoughts, 'The Lord knows our thoughts, that they are but an empty breath',[111] and our desires, 'In regard to the desires of the flesh, we must believe that God is always present to us, as the prophet says to our Lord, "O Lord, all my desire is before Thee."' This fact is to be not merely believed but impressed upon our minds; a solemn, inescapable reality in which we 'live and move and have our being',[112] and which to forget is the first step toward neglect. It is to be the background of our lives, as a man's love for wife and family, though not always consciously referred to, yet forms the motive which sets in motion and inspires all that he does. To despise God, in whose presence we must inescapably live, must surely be some kind of hell. Who would admit the charge of being guilty of despising God? Hardly anyone, yet this is precisely what disobeying his commands means, for in so doing we question or deny his rights, we treat him as of no consequence, arrogate to ourselves that place he alone rightly holds.

Let us, then, reflect upon this, but also upon the fact 'that life everlasting is prepared for them that fear him'. The supreme reason for fearing God is simply that he is God, but this does not lessen the truth that it is by fearing him that we shall come to him, for the fear of the Lord, says holy Scripture, is not only the beginning but the crown and the fullness of wisdom. There is no way to God, who is our final and complete reward, save that of walking before him, as he said to Abraham, 'Walk before me, and be perfect'.[113] And who, knowing God to be what he is, and desiring him as the end which he is, would not walk fearfully, carefully, obediently, 'keeping [themselves] at all times from sin and vice', whether of the thoughts, the tongue, the eyes, the hands, the feet, or the individual will, hastening to cut off the desires of the flesh lest by any of these we be led from the right way, and lose that vision of God which is vouchsafed alone to the pure in heart? 'Let us be on our guard, then, against evil desires, since death has its seat close to the entrance of delight', a phrase as striking as it is true.

This first degree of humility cannot stand alone, but needs the strong support and directing force of the will. 'The second degree is that [we] love not [our] own will, nor delight in gratifying [our] own desires, but carry out in [our] actions that saying of the Lord, "I came not to do my own will, but the will of him who sent me."'[114] Nothing is clearer than that neither the initial fear of God, of the divine anger and the consequences of sin, nor the desire of heaven is sufficient to cause us to forsake and overcome the desires of our lower nature. No instinct in humanity is stronger than self-preservation, yet, strong as it is, it is no match for the pull of the passions. Nor will even the mind's sight of good suffice unless the will is constrained to vigorous action against the desires which would make it captive. We have spoken already of what is meant by one's own will, ever turned toward self-gratification, and here the emphasis is laid on the necessity of carrying out in action that which the fear of God imposes upon us. Wishing, desiring, hoping, these by themselves are useless; we must act, and in acting discover that we can do what hesitation and parleying with the enemy will succeed only in weakening and convincing us is impossible. Let us reply to every temptation, 'I can do all things through Christ who strengthens me,'[115] and do what is required of us, in the power of him 'who pleased not himself'[116] but in all things bent his human will in obedience to the will of his heavenly Father.

With this in mind it is natural that St Benedict should make the third degree of humility consist in 'that a man for the love of God submit himself in obedience to his superior, imitating the Lord, of whom the Apostle saith: "He was made obedient, even unto death."' Now, not to the monk alone is the divine will made known through superiors, nor is obedience merely a virtue of religious. Christ our Lord speaks to each one through his church, in the pages of holy Scripture, through those who, in one degree or another, are set over us. The example of our Lord in rendering obedience to Mary and Joseph, to the Jewish church, to the civil authority, pagan as it was, and the repeated injunctions of the apostles to the first converts to the faith, establish the need of such obedience beyond all question. 'The liberty wherewith Christ has made us free',[117] far from liberating us from obedience, has made it more necessary and understandable. It is by a rational, willed, Christian obedience, teaches St

Peter, that we are to live honestly among the Gentiles, that they, seeing our good works, may 'glorify God in the day of visitation'.[118] Therefore 'for the Lord's sake accept the authority of every human institution . . . for it is God's will that by doing right you should silence the ignorance of the foolish. As servants of God, live as free people, yet do not use your freedom as a pretext for evil'.[119] Children, servants, wives, all people, are exhorted to obedience. 'And all of you must clothe yourselves with humility in your dealings with one another, for "God opposes the proud, but gives grace to the humble."'[120]

SATURDAY IN PASSIONTIDE

Humility – III

To have surmounted the first three rungs of the ladder of humility is to have accomplished – or to be on the way to accomplishing – the hardest part of our ascent. It is the end of the purgative way in which the passions are set at rest, the will surrendered, the whole being set in obedience to and imitation of our divine Master. But we are not yet at the summit, and must see what the next steps bring us, not, as we have said, exactly as St Benedict expects of his sons, but as they are expected of all Christians, each in the way and manner consonant with our particular vocation.

St Benedict, in outlining the fourth degree of humility, speaks still of obedience, but now of that which demands 'hard and contrary things, nay, even injuries' done to one, which, he says, should be embraced patiently and with a quiet mind, so that we 'do not grow weary or give in, for the Scripture says: "[Whoever] shall persevere unto the end shall be saved"[121] and again "Let thy heart take courage, and wait thou upon the Lord"'.[122]

Now let us be quite clear that the saint is not asking one whit more than do our Lord and his apostles. There is nothing in the life and teaching of Jesus and his saints which leads us to expect an easy, comfortable life free from 'hard and contrary things', nor any doubt as to how they would have us meet and deal with them. In order to follow our Lord we are to deny ourselves, and take up our cross; and whatever that cross may be, it has a resemblance to the hard, rough wood of the cross upon which he suffered. 'In this world you will have trouble',[123] hatred, persecution, mockery, and in all this to look for, and find, blessing. 'Blessed are you when people revile you and persecute you and utter all kinds of evil against you falsely on my account. Rejoice and be glad, for your reward is great in heaven.'[124]

We in this country have lived so long in peace, so far as our religion is concerned, that we have come almost to believe that such things belonged only to the past. But were we more conversant with what has been going on in our own time in other countries, we might have found it less easy to lapse into complacency. And we may well reflect upon the fact that if for some centuries we have been among the relatively few people who have not been persecuted, but treated with tolerance followed by indifference, this is due not to our witness to the faith but to our easygoing and compromising acquiescence in it.

However, it is not of persecution that St Benedict is thinking, but of such 'hard and contrary things and injuries' as are met with, in some form or another, in every Christian life, which, he says are 'to be embraced patiently and with a quiet mind', or we might read, 'in silent acceptance'. And his meaning cannot be better illustrated and driven home than by the words of St Peter: 'For it is a credit to you if, being aware of God, you endure pain while suffering unjustly. If you endure when you are beaten for doing wrong, what credit is that? But if you endure when you do right and suffer for it, you have God's approval. For to this you have been called, because Christ also suffered for you, leaving you an example, so that you should follow in his steps.'[125]

The sufferings, trials, temptations, and injuries which come to us under the providence of God are to be met, not merely with that resignation which often only disguises an inward rebellion, and a feeling of martyrdom undeserved. They are to be embraced as opportunities, by our response to which we may grow in humility, patience and the practice of forgiveness. And it is in thus welcoming them that we shall deprive them of that bitterness which otherwise they cause within us. 'Grasp the nettle and it will not sting,' says the proverb, and how many an enemy has been overcome by being treated as a friend, as on that memorable occasion when Totila, King of the Goths, in his raid upon Italy, was met by St Benedict, who so spoke to him that as St Gregory relates, 'The king, hearing these things, was wonderfully afraid, and desiring the holy man to commend him to God, departed; and from that time forward was nothing so cruel as he had been before'.

'To be embraced patiently', for, says the saint elsewhere, 'by patience we share in the passion of Christ', and St John speaks of himself as 'your companion in the patience of Jesus',[126] whilst the Christians in Ephesus are praised for their endurance, patience, and labour for Christ, in which they have not fainted; and to the church in Thyatira it is said, 'I know your works – your love, faith, service, and patient endurance';[127] and to that of Philadelphia, 'Because you have kept my word of patient endurance, I will keep you from the hour of trial that is coming on the whole world'.[128] Of this virtue we must speak later, since by it our Lord declares 'we possess our souls',[129] and St Paul teaches us that 'the object of tribulations is to develop patience; and patience, experience; and experience, hope; which does not disappoint us',[130] and St James, that 'the testing of your faith produces patience, but let patience be effective, that you may be mature and whole, lacking nothing'.

'With a quiet mind', which does not break out against 'the slings and arrows of outrageous fortune', nor suffer itself to be fussed, distracted, and put out by them, knowing that, as says à Kempis, 'all our peace in this . . . life must be placed in humble endurance rather than in absence of contradiction'; and speaking of temptations, 'By flight alone we cannot overcome; but by patience and true humility we become stronger than all our enemies.'

So 'shall we not grow weary or given in' by impatience, opening ourselves to the influence of those things which daily come upon us for our strengthening and perfecting;

but they will so benefit us only as we bear them patiently, 'enduring to the end', even as our Lord 'endured the cross, despising the shame, and was set down at the right hand of God'.[131] For here is 'the patience of the saints'.[132]

Palm Sunday

Humility – IV

The degrees of humility which follow are primarily concerned with various ways in which a religious should exercise this virtue. But amongst them we may find much which, in degree and manner, is applicable to all Christians.

'The fifth degree of humility is to hide from the abbot none of the evil thoughts which beset one's heart, nor the sins committed in secret, but humbly to confess them.' St Benedict is not speaking here of sacramental confession (which, like so much of Christian faith and practice, he takes for granted) but of the opening of one's heart to the abbot, who represents Christ in the monastery, outside the sacrament of Penance which, in the case of St Benedict and other early abbots, lay outside their power as they were not priests.

This practice of confessing, not only our sins but our temptations, is recommended to all by the directors of the spiritual life, and is of value both because the thought of doing it helps to check the temptation and because the priest may be able to give advice as to how to deal with it in ways of which the penitent is ignorant. Moreover it strikes at that deep instinct within us to 'keep ourselves to ourselves', which is often due to pride, to shame, and to the fear of being known for what we really are. Nor should we forget that in such an unfolding of our evil thoughts we get so much nearer to the hidden roots of sin than is often made known in the confession of the actual sins themselves.

'The sixth degree of humility is for a monk to be contented with the meanest and worst of everything.' The Christian must learn, with St Paul, 'in every state to be content',[133] and as he teaches, 'having food and clothing, let us be content',[134] and, 'be content with what you have',[135] that our manner of life 'be without covetousness'.[136] For, not many possessions, whether of the mind or of worldly things, 'but godliness with contentment is great gain'.[137] We need not *seek* the 'meanest and worst of everything', but to be content with what we have, or what we may honestly gain, and is suitable to our vocation and station, is the only way in which true happiness is to be found. It is to be noted, that in the chapter on the Clothes of the Brethren St Benedict says that the abbot is to 'be careful about their size' and that they 'fit well', and also, that for those monks who go on a journey cowls and tunics be provided 'a little better than they usually wear'.

Let us be wise as Agur the son of Jakeh, and pray, 'Remove far from me vanity and lies: give me neither poverty nor riches; feed me with food convenient for me: lest I be full, and deny thee, saying, Who is the Lord? or lest I be poor, and steal, and take the name of my God in vain.' Or even still wiser, and with St Ignatius Loyola, seek for that indifference and detachment in 'regard to all created things – in all that is left to the liberty of our free choice, and is not forbidden it – so that we do not wish for health rather than sickness, for riches rather than poverty, for honour rather than ignominy, for long life rather than a short one, and so in all other matters, desiring solely and choosing only those things which may better lead us to the end for which we were created'. We recall, too, St Francis de Sales' 'Ask nothing, refuse nothing', with regard to temporal things.

'The seventh degree of humility is that he should not only call himself with his tongue lower and viler than all, but also believe himself with inmost affection of heart to be so, humbling himself, and saying with the psalmist, "I am a worm, and no man, the shame of men, and the outcast of the people: I have been exalted, and cast down, and confounded."'

[There can now surely be few who would not recognise that the quotation cited by St Benedict is taken out of context. This psalm, an 'individual lament', is written from the tormented heart of one who is enduring such suffering as can be expressed in no other way. As an individual lament, it was never intended to be universally adopted as the religious person's personal manifesto. The psalmist is expressing not remorse for sin but despair in the face of unimaginable suffering and the sense of being abandoned by God. Hopefully, then, it is not a psalm which speaks into the day-to-day life and discipleship of most of us.]

[The positive aspect of St Benedict's use of this text, however, is with regard to our perception of ourselves in relation to those around us. It is dangerously easy to set ourselves up as the measure by which we judge others who, since our self-assessment is by definition hardly impartial, are harshly judged indeed. St Benedict calls us to an other- rather than self-centred view of the world, recognising first all that is good in other people and responding to what we perceive as their shortcomings primarily with a recognition that whatever virtues we have are gifts of God and not our own possessions.]

We should compare what we are, not with other people but with what we were created to be and, had we used God's gifts diligently, we ought and might have been. Then, indeed, we shall be driven to confess, in thinking of those whom we consider to be suffering the temporal punishment of sin, to say, 'There, but for the grace of God, go I.'

'The eighth degree of humility is for a monk to do nothing except what is authorised by the common Rule of the monastery, or the example of seniors.'

Self-assertion, eccentricity, gratuitous contempt for the common conventions of society, are all contrary to the spirit of Christ, who, in St Paul's words, made himself of no reputation, and took upon him the form of a servant, and was made in human likeness[138] – one of the crowd, we might say – and who, although undeniably formidable and rigorous in debate, never attempted to belittle others in order to gratify his own ego or to court publicity by sensationalism. Singularity is no sign of sanctity, even if some of the saints have indulged in it, and is nowhere more out of place than in the sanctuary. The common rule of the church is sufficient for all, and if it is added to it should be by direction or approval, not merely by self-will, and then, as is too often the case, made a standard by which others are judged.

MONDAY IN HOLY WEEK

Humility – V

The next three degrees of humility are concerned with the guard of the tongue, excessive laughter, and with that fitting moderation of speech which, says the saint, should be gentle, humble, grave, 'with few and reasonable words', and not of a noisy character.

One of the most profitable ways of studying holy Scripture is to take a particular subject, and to see what the sacred writers – 'holy people of God', as St Peter names them, 'moved by the Holy Spirit'[139] – have to say about it. Such study is bound to be illuminating, and is often disconcerting, not least when the subject chosen is that of the use of speech.

The words of our Lord come at once to mind. 'I tell you, on the day of judgment you will have to give an account for every careless word you utter; for by your words you will be justified, and by your words you will be condemned.'[140] The Preacher warns us, 'Never be rash with your mouth, nor let your heart be quick to utter a word before God, for God is in heaven and you upon earth; therefore let your words be few . . . a fool's voice [comes] with many words.'[141] Here the reference is to words uttered in worship and prayer, and we shall recall our Lord's saying that we are not heard for our much speaking, but, as St Benedict reminds us, 'for our purity of heart and tears of compunction'. The book of Proverbs will tell us that 'When words are many, transgression is not lacking',[142] that 'one that useth many words shall be abhorred', that 'one who spares words is knowledgeable',[143] and 'Do you see someone who is hasty in speech? There is more hope for a fool than for anyone like that'.[144] And if we need any further confirmation of the need of guarding our tongues, we shall find it in the Letter of St James: 'And the tongue is a fire. The tongue is placed among our members as a world of iniquity; it stains the whole body, sets on fire the cycle of nature, and is itself set on fire by hell . . . a restless evil, full of deadly poison.'[145] Who of us is there who cannot see how much harm we have done to ourselves and to others, how much mischief and sin we have caused by our idle, malicious, detracting, whispering, slanderous, foolish, backbiting, envious, lying words? Who will not blush at the memory of their exaggerations, their repetitions of mere rumours, the facile judgements pronounced without knowledge of the facts, the hours spent in gossiping, rarely without sin, the cruelty of words, with which the approval or laughter of other people was sought? And what does all this betray but what we are within, for 'out of the abundance of the heart the mouth speaks'.[146]

'Let all evil speaking be put away from you,' writes St Paul. 'Lay aside all guile, envies, and evil speaking,'[147] says St Peter. 'Let everyone be slow to speak,'[148] writes St James.

St Benedict speaks more than once of excessive laughter, by which he means loud, vulgar, ill-mannered, contemptuous laughter, not that of a merry heart such as the psalmist speaks of, 'Then was our mouth filled with laughter, and our tongue with joy',[149] but 'that excessive laughter' which, says the book of Proverbs, 'shows what a person is'. There is joy in heaven, and the greatest of Christian poets does not hesitate to speak of that 'Light eternal' which is the Blessed Trinity, as 'smiling at thine own intents', of 'thousands of jocund angels', and of that Queen, 'beauty that was bliss', who smiled upon their games and at their song.

> Seemed what I witnessed with so deep delight
> a laughter of the universe; for this
> elation entered through both ear and sight.

And who has better cause to laugh than Christians who are at one with the source of all happiness and joy, and who thus should perceive at what and how we may laugh without sin?

Moderation, discretion, a simple, humble, befitting gravity, these are virtues which characterise the whole of the Holy Rule, and are as necessary in the world as in the cloister. Our speech, says the saint, should be gentle, humble, grave, quiet, our words 'few and reasonable', and such indeed is the speech of Christian gentlemen and gentlewomen to whatever social sphere they belong.

What horrors our noisy, blatant, self-advertising, vulgar world might have been saved from had Christians remembered this. But no; we must for ever be talking, chattering like monkeys in a tropical jungle; we are immoderate and indiscreet in speech, anxious to air our own opinions and judgements, without ever asking ourselves, or taking trouble to find out, whether they are true or reasonable; loud and noisy in speech; rude and discourteous to those whom, God forgive us, we esteem 'beneath ourselves'; and all this because we have never sought to become 'meek and humble of heart', as our Saviour bade us learn of him.

In the last degree of humility St Benedict again emphasises the truth that true humility must, and will, manifest itself in our exterior life, words, and conduct. Wherever they are, in whatever task they are engaged, humble people will, without knowing it, or seeking to display it, 'show [their] humility to all who see [them]'. Our Lord has bidden us, 'Let your light so shine before others, that they may see your good works, and glorify your Father who is in heaven'[150] – not you who are upon earth. 'Let your light shine.' Not 'Wave your light about', but let it shine as any light must simply, naturally, of its own power. And for this, there must not be that in the exterior which, like grime upon a window, hinders the light from shining through.

'Having, therefore, ascended all these degrees of humility, the monk (and the Christian) will presently arrive at that love of God which, being perfect, casteth out fear; whereby he shall begin to keep, without labour, and as it were naturally, and by custom, all those precepts which he had hitherto observed not without fear, no longer through dread of hell, but for the love of Christ, and of a good habit and delight in virtue. Which thing God will vouchsafe to manifest by the Holy Spirit in his labourer, now cleansed from vice and sin.' Thus does the saint conclude this chapter on humility.

TUESDAY IN HOLY WEEK

Humility – VI

The fact that an ideal is above our heads is no reason for not striving after it, much less for abandoning it because it continues to be out of our immediate reach. Actually, what God desires of us is not attainment, which is his gift, but endeavour, by which we become capable of receiving that gift. 'I do not ask of my servants success, but only an infinite desire', and such a desire cannot be fully satisfied in this life. 'Blessed are they who hunger and thirst after righteousness; for they shall be filled.'[151] Filled with what? 'All the fullness of God,'[152] the Apostle tells us and that is not possible in this present life, however near we may come to it. For satisfaction, attainment, success in this life is full of danger, so rarely is human nature capable of sustaining it without abusing it, or settling down in a contentment with what has been achieved, only to lose what has been gained.

Christians may be idealists but we must be realists, for what we have to face, and deal with, are not pious and beautiful dreams, or visions invoked by sentiment, but facts, realities, unalterable and inescapable, which demand a rational approach and appreciation, and a realistic response in action. The Christian way of life does not lead by sunlit meadows and still waters to a lotus-eaters' paradise, nor will those who walk therein be fed with virtues, as Elijah with bread from heaven. It is the way of disciples, who have to learn hard lessons; of workers who must learn their craft; of labourers who must be prepared for toil and weariness, and often to seeing very little for their pains; of pilgrims before whom loom high hills and long, winding, tiresome roads, and foul as well as fine weather; of soldiers on active service, whose courage and endurance will be tested to the utmost, and who must not shrink from danger, nor whimper when they are wounded.

The consideration of what St Benedict teaches about humility will probably convince us that we have scarcely put our feet on the first rung of the ladder, and the way in which it towers above our heads may discourage us. If it were only shorter, or easier to mount, but as it is . . .

Now, when such thoughts come into our minds they must be dismissed at once. We must never become defeatists. Whatever the position and the difficulties may be, however incapable we seem to be, there is only one thing in the Christian life which must be done always, and that is to go on. If, says St Benedict, there are things which are difficult, 'do not therefore fly in dismay from the way of salvation', 'never despair of God's mercy', 'for as we go forward in our life and faith, we shall, with hearts enlarged, and unspeakable sweetness of love, run in the way of God's commandments'.

You say, 'I am very far indeed from being humble.' Well, that you know it is a good sign; what would be disturbing would be for you to think you were humble. 'It is better,' writes Dom Chapman, 'to doubt about oneself and walk about in the dark, than to be pleased with oneself; for fear of having the least touch of the Pharisee'; and as for 'feelings', he says, 'Of course we can be saints without feeling we are pigs.'

The real point is, Have I got the right idea of what humility consists in? Am I taking pains to be humble? Am I using the means by which alone humility is gained? We must walk before we can run, and learn before we can exercise knowledge, and, above all, we must desire earnestly, and seek continually, any virtue we would gain. Listen to St Francis de Sales, 'Shall I be humble? Yes, if you will it. But I do will it. Then you are humble. But I feel distinctly that I am not. So much the better, for this makes it more certain.'

The means by which we may become humble are abundant, common, and daily within our reach. Since God loves and esteems humility so highly as not only to regard it in his handmaiden, but also to humble himself by becoming human, we may be sure that he will help us when we ask him for this grace. But let us remember that his answer to our prayer comes in two ways: first in bestowing the grace which enlightens us and strengthens us in our desire and resolve to become humble, and secondly in providing the means by which we may actually become so. And these are the many and various things and happenings which cause humiliation, the best of which are not such as we seek and impose upon ourselves, but which come to us in the ordinary course of our daily lives.

This last fact is one of the hardest we have to face, for we are all inclined to seek God's gifts in our own way. We desire humility, but want to choose our own ways of becoming humble, which is but evidence of self-regard and vanity. There are two ways only of gaining humility. One is by seeing it in Jesus, and learning it from him. 'Learn of me, for I am meek and humble of heart.'[153] The other, which is as necessary, is to train ourselves to accept and say 'Thank you' for all the daily humiliations which come to us, whether they be reproofs or snubs, deserved or undeserved, unpleasant tasks, our own imperfections and failures, being ignored, having our 'rights' trodden upon, our cherished opinions scoffed at, our comfort disturbed, and a score of similar things. 'Observe,' says St Teresa, 'that we gain more in a single day by trials which come to us from God and our neighbour than we should in ten thousand years by penances and exercises we take upon ourselves.' It is God, not we, who sets up and forms the rungs of the ladder by which we come to him only by becoming like him.

WEDNESDAY IN HOLY WEEK

Patience – I

'By patience we share in the Passion of Christ.' This is one of the most beautiful sentences which St Benedict penned in the Holy Rule, revealing as it does the truth that patience is one of the surest ways by which we are made one with, and share in, the redeeming passion of our Lord, and indeed in the divine life itself, for 'God is patient because he is eternal' and the Apostle prays that 'the God of patience and consolation grant you to be like-minded one toward another.'

The saint has spoken already of that patience of God which 'waits daily for us to respond by our deeds to his holy admonitions', since his will is that 'all should be saved, and come to the knowledge of the truth', and of the need of our bearing patiently any wrong done to us. But here he goes to the very root of the matter. Christians, says St Paul, are 'co-operators with God'. Our vocation is to continue on earth the life and labour and passion of Jesus, in whom God's work is revealed and accomplished, according to the words of our Lord, 'I have finished the work you gave me to do.'[154] And in no way are Christians so completely co-operators with God as when they share in, and so extend, the passion of their divine master. And it does not need much thought to see how in the passion all the patience which Jesus manifests in his life on earth comes to its perfect fulfilment, and shines forth in both his bearing and his words. 'Thy life,' says à Kempis, 'is our way, and by holy patience we come to thee', who did come down from heaven, and take our miseries, that we might learn patience.

All spiritual writers insist upon the fact that every form of impatience is injurious to the Christian life. St Francis de

Sales calls it 'the mother imperfection of all imperfections' and tells us that 'we must possess our hearts in longanimity; great designs are not effected save by the virtue of patience, and the passage of time.' All impatience dissipates our life, wastes our energy, prevents our seeing clearly, causes us to lose our balance, leads us to act in the wrong way or at the wrong time, to say things we do not mean and may lead us to acts and decisions which cannot be recalled, and which bear consequences we never dreamt of. Impatience always betrays a lack of faith, humility, charity, and confidence in God. 'In your patience,' says our Lord, 'you shall possess your souls,'[155] be master of yourselves, whereas impatience is a loss of ourselves, by which we become unhappy slaves. 'Woe unto you that have lost patience! what will ye do when the Lord shall visit you?'

It may sound foolish to speak of impatience with God, yet it is a common fault of which even children today are guilty, having, no doubt, learnt it from their parents. How impatient we are with the necessity of walking by faith, and not by sight! 'Impatience for vision is one of the last faults to be cured,' says Coventry Patmore. 'Why all this mystery about religion?' asked a child recently, evidently under the impression that there were no mysteries in the physical order, and little realising what a mystery we are to ourselves. How restless and impatient we get when our prayers are not answered at once, or in the way we had expected. Why doesn't God do something? we ask petulantly, when we should ask, Why do not I do something? We are all for haste, for quick returns, for spectacular results, and are irked at the slowness, the incredible patience of God, the way in which he permits evils to go on, seems to be content to endure what to flesh and blood is almost unendurable. But what is all this but to forget what we should be were God to lose patience with us? To forget also that so many of the trials we complain of are allowed by God to go on because we have refused to learn the lessons they were designed to teach us. How few people, if we may judge from what is said and written about war, seem to have the slightest idea of the fundamental causes which bring it about, and what it ought to teach us, truths which are plain enough in holy Scripture, even if neither politicians nor the press dare to utter them.

St James bids us consider 'the patience of Job',[156] and most people would say that it consisted in the way in which he bore his losses, his afflictions, and the well-meant but boring attempts of his friends to console him. But he does not, as a matter of fact, exhibit any great patience with these things. The real point lies much deeper. He had been brought up to believe, as did his friends, that suffering was always the consequence of sin on the part of sufferers, as prosperity was of their righteousness, a theory still held by many, as by the Puritans who regarded poverty as a sign of God's displeasure, so that, as Tawney has said, 'A society which reverences the attainment of riches as the supreme felicity will naturally be disposed to regard the poor as damned in the next world, if only to justify itself for making their life a hell in this .' Job sees that this theory is wrong. He is not conscious that he has sinned in such ways as deserve such misery. Later, when God speaks, he comes to know better, but all through the book his complaint is that he has served God for naught. The temptation comes, 'What is the good, why not curse God and die?'[157] No, that is the one thing he will not do. He cannot understand; he is, as we should say, thoroughly 'fed up'; but 'though he slay me, yet will I put my trust in him'.[158] And that trust, that patience even in impatience, that resolution to 'wait upon the Lord' is rewarded by a new knowledge of God, and a consequent penitence on Job's part. 'I had heard of you by the hearing of the ear' – and much of what he had heard was untrue – 'but now my eye sees you; therefore I despise myself, and repent in dust and ashes.'[159] For of humility is patience born, and both of such a knowledge of God as will make us exclaim, 'I lay my hand upon my mouth,'[160] and even in the darkest hour 'wait patiently for the Lord'.[161]

Maundy Thursday

Patience – II

Jesus is our model, but a model is of no use unless it is studied and imitated. Have we ever seriously studied, gazed upon, the patience of Jesus by which he reflected on earth the eternal patience of heaven? And if not, how shall we learn to be patient with people, with happenings, with temptations, with our human frailty, with injuries and persecutions?

Think of that patience of Jesus in which he, the Infinite and Eternal Word, embraced with our humanity all the conditions, surroundings and circumstances of a human life. Of the restraining and subjecting of his divine personality to the narrow limitations of his sacred humanity, of the patience which 'did not abhor the Virgin's womb' in which he lay during the nine months, which submitted to the swaddling clothes of infancy and to the slow growth of his human nature, which learnt as we learn, in human fashion, taught by parents and teachers, he, the very Truth itself. Consider the patience of the thirty years at Nazareth where, as a humble carpenter, Jesus lived and worked and waited for the hour decreed by his eternal Father, as if nothing mattered but to do the common tasks of each day as it came. The patience with the circumstances which surrounded his public mission, the ignorance and fickleness of people, the dullness of disciples, the opposition of enemies, the annoyance of relations, the misunderstanding, carping, and criticism, the false accusations, the little results. His patience with sinners, with the woman of Samaria, with her who was taken in adultery, with Mary Magdalene, with Judas and with Peter. His patience under temptation, in prayer, in unceasing labour, in suffering, upon the cross. A patience enduring, inexhaustible – who knows it better than ourselves? – exercised under conditions similar to those in which, in some degree or another, we are called upon to follow the example of his patience.

Do we complain about, or fret under, or rage impatiently with, our limitations, real or imaginary, seeing the conditions under which we live, the work we have to do, as bars of a prison cell from which there is no apparent escape? Then, so long as these must be borne, why make them worse by impatience and murmuring, breeding in ourselves a spirit of sullen discontent which would poison any freedom we might attain? 'Whatever [we] cannot amend in [ourselves], or in others, [we] ought to bear with patience until God ordain otherwise,' says à Kempis. Things do not get better by our railing at them, nor do we; but they do become different when we accept them and learn to praise God with them. Or, do we give way to discontent with our own limitations of soul or body, envying those who seem to be more fortunate than ourselves? But this effects nothing good, whereas if we set ourselves patiently to use what we have, instead of dreaming what we would do with what we have not, we should discover how much richer we were than we had believed.

How do we react to the thousand and one things which come to pass daily in our life in the world? The interruptions, the demands made upon us, the opposition we encounter, the disappointments, the misunderstanding the criticisms, the people who try us, the annoyances, the monotony of doing the same things over and over again, the occasions when duties crowd upon us, and things happen 'all of a heap' as we say? Well, impatience will not help, any more than it does when we are trying to disentangle a tightly knotted piece of string. But patience will; for, as says St Catherine of Genoa, 'It always conquers and is never overcome'.

What of our patience with those who, from ignorance or malice, sin against us? With those who, like the Samaritan woman, love to argue about religion rather than practise it; with those whom we catch in the act of sin – what if we were so caught? – with those who deny us in our time of need or, worse, betray us to our enemies; with those whom we have been patient with so long, but now we say, 'My patience is exhausted'? But is there any reason on our side why God should not say it of us?

Do we try and overcome temptations by the exercise of patient endurance of them (often the only way they can be overcome)? Are we learning to be patient with ourselves? 'The best practice of patience is the bearing of oneself in failure and feebleness of will,' says St Jane Frances de Chantal. Do we know 'the value of patience in prayer', how to 'wait patiently for the Lord' till he hear our calling? Or what we lose by dragging our impatience, our lust for doing and results, disturbing the peace of God with the fussy haste of the world? 'Rest in the Lord, wait patiently for him', 'for the vision is yet for an appointed time; though it tarry, wait for it'.

By patience we 'attempt an humble, creaturely imitation of the eternal, spaceless Creator, under the deliberately accepted conditions of time and space'. It is the condition of our perseverance, as of all great, heroic, worthwhile things. When we read the stories of people's attempts to accomplish what seems humanly impossible, we are stirred by the thought of the glory, the thrill, the wonder of it all. But how different was the reality! The exercise of a ceaseless, dull, painful, monotonous patience, with circumstances, setbacks, failures, and, not least, the learning how to live together in daily companionship with others, especially when this meant long periods doing next to nothing, as Captain Scott records in his diary, and yet without the slightest tension amongst the heroic members of the expedition.

'Do not lessen thy crown by impatience.' The race we are called to run is not to the swift, but to those who, 'looking to Jesus',[162] run with patience the race set before them, constantly keeping in mind 'him that endured such contradiction of sinners against himself' lest they 'be wearied and faint in mind', and so share not in the strength of the passion of Christ.

Good Friday

Silence

The sixth chapter of the Rule is entitled *De Taciturnate*, the English equivalent of which, taciturnity, hardly conveys the sense of the Latin which does not imply any sullenness or self-centredness, but the spirit and habit of silence. And there could not be a better day in which to consider this than that upon which the 'despised and rejected by the world'[163] was oppressed and afflicted, 'yet he opened not his mouth: he is brought as a lamb to the slaughter, and as a sheep before her shearers is silent, so he opened not his mouth'.[164]

Seven times he spoke, seven words of love:
And all three hours his silence cried
for mercy on the souls of men.

For of him it is written, 'Here is my servant, whom I uphold, my chosen, in whom my soul delights; I have put my spirit upon him; he will bring forth justice to the nations. He will not cry or lift up his voice, or make it heard in the street',[165] and, 'Be silent, O all flesh, before the Lord: for he is raised up out of the habitation of his holiness'.[166]

We have spoken already of the guard of the tongue and here we shall think, not of that exterior silence, which befits the Christian in this noisy, blatant, boastful, chattering world, but of that interior silence which is a necessary condition of spiritual life and activity. That silence of the mind, of the memory, of the imagination and of the passions, which is the foundation of all true worship, reverence, and prayer, and of which St John of the Cross says, 'That which we most need in order to make progress is to be silent before God, with the desire and with the tongue, for the language he best hears is the silent language of love.'

Silence of the mind, kept as an enclosed garden, free from alien intruders who would disturb its peace, occupy its attention, distract its thoughts, fill it with useless rubbish, deprive it of its power of concentration, make it impossible for it to be given wholly to God and to what he desires of us in the way of our vocation.

Silence of the memory, that vast storehouse in whose chambers are lodged the records of the past, things heard, seen, and done, good and evil, precious and worthless, any of which may come to remembrance in moments when they are least welcome, and which we need to sort out, retaining only those which are for our good, whether it be such remembrance of past sin as shall stir us to deeper penitence, or of the mercies of God, moving us to praise and thankfulness.

Silence of the imagination, that splendid and dangerous faculty by which our thoughts take material form and shape, become vivid, stirring pictures, the appeal of which will sweep our will into consent of evil, unless they are silenced and blotted out in the first moment when they begin to take form.

Silence of the passions, those turbulent movements of the lower part of the soul, ever striving to dominate our lives; good servants only as they are kept in their place, the accomplishing of which is the main effort of the beginnings of Christian life, when by detachment from the desires they evoke we strive to set our house in order, and so to come to that moment which St John of the Cross speaks of in the first lines of the poem upon which he founds the early books of the *Ascent of Mount Carmel.*

> On a dark night, kindled with yearning love,
> O happy chance! I went forth unobserved,
> my house being now at rest.

Few of us can hope to find silence, quietude, peace, in the world in which our lot is cast, and in which one of our most real dangers is the spirit and love of noise, of crowds, of speed and excitement, with which it is so easy to become infected. We cannot even escape from it in public worship, indeed many seem to think that a service in which no organ blares, no loud voices, whether of priest or people, are raised, is scarcely worthy of the name. Even the quiet spaces of silence which the church has allowed for in the liturgy must be filled with hymns which, too often, have little to do with what is being done at the altar, and should be done by the people. We have grown afraid of silence, do not know what to do with it, cannot be trusted to use it, but must be given something easier to do, lest we get into mischief. It is the same with our prayer, which we imagine is not prayer unless we are talking all the time, forgetful of such words as 'Be still, and know that I am God',[167] 'It is good that one should both hope and quietly wait for the salvation of the Lord',[168] 'In quietness and confidence shall be your strength',[169] 'The Lord is in his holy heaven, let all the earth keep silence before him'.[170] Even on Good Friday we are not content simply to be in the silent company who stand beneath the cross, and into whose silent hearts drop the precious words from the depths of the Sacred Heart of Jesus, there to find more response than all that evoked by the sermons, often full of other things, and the hymns of the Three Hours' devotion which delight our sentimentalism.

'Aspire to be quiet,'[171] says the Apostle; 'Seek peace and pursue it,'[172] the psalmist; 'I have need to busy my heart with quietude,' the modem poet. Our worship, our prayer, our whole life would be better and more fruitful if it were more governed by the spirit of silence, in which, with St Augustine, we might say, 'Mine own soul being still, may it be transformed, not by thinking upon myself, but upon Thee, my God,' and with Sister Elizabeth of the Trinity, 'I want to be all silence, all adoration, that I may penetrate more deeply into God, and become so full of him that I may give him in my prayer to those poor souls still ignorant of his gift.' But for this, we must learn how to

Sit down, nor turn mine eyes away,
nor speak, nor even pray.
But only look on thee, and wait to hear
thy gentle voice meet my attentive ear.
Lord, I confess I know not anything,
but all my nothingness to thee I bring;
I will subdue my will,
rest in thy Presence, and be still.

Holy Saturday

Peace

We come to that 'holy Easter' which St Benedict bids us await with 'the joy of spiritual longing', to the return of our victor King from the dark portal of death and hell, that he may bestow upon us his blessing of peace, as on that first Easter he uttered his 'Peace be with you' to the hearts of his sad and troubled disciples.

Pax is the Benedictine motto, and it may be with some surprise that, at first sight, there is next to nothing about peace in the Holy Rule. The psalmist's 'Seek peace and pursue it'[173] is quoted; one of the Instruments of Good Works is, 'Not to make a feigned peace'; and another, 'To make peace with an adversary before the sun sets'; and that is all. But the whole purpose of every chapter of the Rule is to establish the individual, and so the community, in peace: that peace which can be attained only by a struggle against its enemies.

The early chapters tell us of the things necessary that peace may reign in the individual: the return to the God of peace; the taking up of 'the weapons of obedience' in order to fight for our true King; prayer, service, the hearing and doing of the will of God; faith and confidence; the war against evil thoughts; humility, good works, silence. Then we come to those things by which peace is to be secured in the community: the ordering of the divine Office; the description of the kind of people who should be chosen for positions of authority, from the abbot to the doorkeeper; the care to be taken in admitting candidates, and in training them; the ordering of daily duties; the care of the sick, the aged, and of children; the rules about food, drink, sleep, and clothing; the constant reference to the need of courtesy, forbearance, patience, kindness, forgiveness; the treatment of the poor who come as guests, to whom 'special care and solicitude is to be shown because in them Christ is more received'; the good zeal and charity which should be shown by all, so that in nothing may any one 'be troubled or grieved in the house of God'.

The Holy Rule, indeed, lays down the principles and practices which are as necessary to secure peace in the home and in society as in a monastery. All people, whatever station they occupy in the world, may here learn how to live and conduct themselves as members of the family of God, and so contribute to that peace which is 'the tranquillity of order'.

'My peace I give unto you,' says our Lord, and from him alone can it be found. But if we are to find it, we must know what it is we are seeking. For this peace is not that of an empty, comfortable inaction; the peace of a stagnant, unruffled pool of water, or of animals feeding in the stillness of a summer afternoon. It is the peace which reigned in the Sacred Heart who lived in occupied territory, in the midst of strife and unrest; the peace of a full, ordered, harmonious, integrated life which, ever replenished at its divine source, flows out in a steady, undiminished stream, spreading peace wherever it comes, a veritable 'river whose streams make glad the city of God'.[174] It is the consequence of an ordered, disciplined life anchored in the will of God *in sua voluntade e nostra pace;* a peace, not to be found in striving, but in abandonment, as, again, Dante says:

> May Thy kingdom's peace
> come unto us; for we, unless it come
> with all our striving, hither tend in vain.

For peace is the arrangement and harmonising of things in relation to their end. Thus we see in a church, in a kitchen, in an office, how everything is arranged and ordered for the particular purpose for which those places and their appointments exist. So is it with the manifold powers and activities of our lives, which, however, being living things, are constantly getting out of their place, quarrelling with each other, so that there can be no peace unless they are put and kept each in its place, which place is determined by the end for which all exist. There can be no peace in a disordered, untidy, dissipated, self-regarding life. 'Order is heaven's first law' and, says St Thomas, 'the best thing in the world'; and St Augustine, 'There is an order which, if we observe it, we shall come to God; if we do not, we shall not come to him.' The whole business of the Christian life is to establish this order within, that so God may bestow his *Pax Vobiscum* upon us.

To do this we must not only set the eyes of our mind upon the pattern shown in the mount, and enter, in worship and prayer, into the sanctuary of the God of peace; we must take care to evict all that would hinder and disturb that peace we seek. We must avoid all haste, disquiet, impatience, anxiety, and fear.

'We must in all things, and everywhere, live peaceably,' says St Francis de Sales. 'If trouble, exterior or interior, come upon us, we must receive it peacefully. If joy comes, we must receive it without excitement. Evil must be avoided peacefully, without disquiet, for otherwise we may fall as we run away. Good must be done peacefully, in haste many faults may be committed. Even our repentance must be made peacefully.' And Père Grou says that if we are to preserve and increase our peace we must treat it as we do good health, enjoy it without thinking about it.

So we come to the end of Lent; and what have we done with it, gained from it? Nothing that is of much value unless we have set our lives more in order, and are determined, at whatever cost, to keep them ordered, and directed toward God. Lent is over, but the holy war goes on; there are no rest-billets for us. We must see that Eastertide aids us to keep what we have gained, and if this is to be so, we must stand armed to defend the citadel of our souls against enemies without and possible traitors within. 'When a strong man, fully armed, guards his castle, his property is safe',[175] 'Stand, therefore, and having done all, stand',[176] firm, resolute, alert, equipped with the whole armour of God. There is no disarmament in the spiritual world.

'Great peace have they who love thy law': the law of love, of truth, of Justice, of order, the divine, eternal law of God upon whom our gaze is to be steadfastly fixed. For 'those of steadfast mind you keep in peace – in peace because they trust in you.'[177]

REFERENCES

References

1 1 Corinthians 3:10 NRSV
2 John 6:68 NRSV
3 Matthew 28:19
4 Luke 10:16
5 Hebrews 3:15
6 Matthew 25:26 NIV
7 Colossians 3:17 NRSV
8 Romans 8:21 NIV
9 2 Corinthians 4:4 NRSV
10 John 9:4 NRSV
11 Acts 17:28
12 John 4:24
13 Acts 17:28
14 James 2:19
15 Hebrews 3:15
16 Mark 4:9 and other refs.
17 John 9:4
18 Hebrews 12:29-29
19 1 John 4:18
20 1 John 3:2 NRSV
21 Matthew 5:48
22 John 1:12 NRSV
23 1 John 3:2 NRSV
24 Matthew 5:8
25 1 Corinthians 13:12
26 1 Corinthians 13:12
27 Colossians 1:15
28 Psalm 19:1
29 John 14:9
30 John 14:7
31 1 John 3:2
32 The monastery is called by St Benedict 'a School of the Lord's Service'
33 Matthew 16:24 NRSV
34 Luke 6:38 NRSV
35 This relates to the vows taken by Benedictines, and is the living of one's life according to the counsels of perfection.
36 Matthew 23:2
37 Matthew 23:3
38 John 8:34-36
39 Matthew 15:19
40 John 14:15
41 Revelation 2:7-10 NRSV
42 Galatians 5:17 NRSV
43 John 18:33
44 John 18:37
45 Revelation 19:16
46 Matthew 28:20
47 Ephesians 6:13 NRSV
48 1 Samuel 16:7 NRSV
49 Matthew 12:34-35
50 Psalm 51:17
51 Philippians 3:12-15 NRSV
52 Psalm 115:1 NRSV
53 1 Corinthians 15:10
54 Hebrews 13:14
55 James 2:17,19
56 Romans 1:5
57 Matthew 28:19
58 Psalm 61:2
59 Matthew 7:24
60 James 2:17
61 John 14:15
62 Matthew 21:31
63 Matthew 25:40 NRSV
64 Matthew 25:40 NRSV
65 John 2:15 NRSV
66 Romans 8:35,37 NRSV
67 King Lear (1605-6) act 5, sc. 3, l.

68 1 John 4:20 NRSV
69 John 8:51 NRSV
70 1 Peter 1:16 NRSV
71 Luke 12:48 NRSV
72 Luke 19:13
73 Acts 3:8
74 Romans 8:21
75 Psalm 115:16
76 Psalm 104:24 NRSV
77 Deuteronomy 8:3; Matthew 4:4, par.
78 John 6:50
79 Revelation 3:15 NRSV
80 Revelation 3:16-17 NRSV
81 Galatians 4:26
82 2 Corinthians 5:1
83 John 14:6
84 Isaiah 35:8 NRSV
85 1 Corinthians 4:10
86 John 8:12
87 Jeremiah 6:16
88 Isaiah 33:17
89 2 Timothy 3:16-17 NRSV
90 Hebrews 1:1
91 2 Peter 1:19 NRSV
92 Mark 9:7
93 John 6:68
94 Luke 11:28
95 Matthew 24:13 NRSV
96 2 Timothy 4:3-4 NRSV
97 Psalm 51:17
98 John 9:4
99 Psalm 31:15
100 Psalm 89:47
101 James 3:14-16 NRSV
102 2 Tim 2:24-25 NRSV
103 Matthew 23:12 NRSV
104 Psalm 131:1 NRSV
105 Psalm 131:2 NRSV
106 Matthew 5:20 NRSV
107 Isaiah 6:5 NRSV
108 Job 42:5-6 NRSV
109 Philippians 2:8 NRSV
110 1 Peter 2:21 NRSV
111 Psalm 94:11 NRSV
112 Acts 17:28
113 Genesis 17:1
114 John 6:38
115 Philippians 4:13
116 Romans 15:3
117 Galatians 5:1
118 1 Peter 2:12
119 1 Peter 2:13, 15-16 NRSV
120 1 Peter 5:5 NRSV
121 Matthew 10:22, par
122 Psalm 27:14
123 John 16:33 NIV
124 Matthew 5:11-12 NRSV
125 1 Peter 2:19-21 NRSV
126 Revelation 1:9
127 Revelation 2:19 NRSV
128 Revelation 3:10 NRSV
129 Luke 21:19
130 Romans 5:3-5
131 Hebrews 12:2
132 Revelation 13:10; 14:12
133 Philippians 4:11
134 1 Timothy 6:8
135 Hebrews 13:5
136 Hebrews 13:5
137 1 Timothy 6:6
138 Philippians 2:7
139 2 Peter 1:21
140 Matthew 12:36-37 NRSV
141 Ecclesiastes 5:2-3 NRSV
142 Proverbs 10:19 NRSV
143 Proverbs 17:27 NRSV
144 Proverbs 29:20 NRSV

145 James 3:6-8 NRSV
146 Matthew 12:34
147 1 Peter 2:1
148 James 1:19
149 Psalm 126:2
150 Matthew 5:16
151 Matthew 5:6
152 Colossians 1:19
153 Matthew 11:29
154 John 17:4
155 Luke 21:19
156 James 5:11
157 Job 2:9
158 Job 13:15
159 Job 42:5-6 NRSV
160 Job 40:4
161 Psalm 40:1
162 Hebrews 12:2
163 Isaiah 53:3
164 Isaiah 53:7
165 Isaiah 42:1-2 NRSV
166 Zechariah 2:13
167 Psalm 46:10
168 Lamentations 3:26
169 Isaiah 30:15
170 Habakkuk 2:20
171 1 Thessalonians 4:11
172 Psalm 34:14
173 Ibid.
174 Psalm 46:4
175 Luke 11:21 NRSV
176 Ephesians 6:13
177 Isaiah 26:3 NRSV